CASTLES
of WALES

CASTLES
of WALES

ALAN PHILLIPS

AMBERLEY

First published as *Castles and Fortifications of Wales*, 2011

This edition first published 2014

Amberley Publishing
The Hill, Stroud
Gloucestershire GL5 4EP

www.amberley-books.com

British Library Cataloguing in Publication Data.
A catalogue record for this book is available from the British Library.

ISBN 978 1 4456 4374 8 (print)
ISBN 978 1 4456 4406 6 (ebook)

Typesetting and Origination by Amberley Publishing.
Printed in Great Britain.

CONTENTS

LIST OF ILLUSTRATIONS

CHAPTER 1

1. The remains of Foel Drygarn hillfort.
2. A stone Roman watchtower at Caerleon.

CHAPTER 2

3. Plan of a typical medieval castle.
4. Sketch of an early motte-and-bailey fortification.
5. A castle walkway at Pembroke Castle.
6. Layout map of Conwy Castle and town in the fourteenth century.

CHAPTER 3

7. Map showing the main castles of Wales.
8. Caernarfon Castle.
9. Caerphilly Castle.
10. Layout plan of Caerphilly Castle.
11. Aerial view of Chepstow Castle.
12. Conwy Castle.
13. Plan of Conwy Castle.
14. Another view of Conwy Castle.
15. Criccieth Castle.
16. Manorbier Castle.
17. Layout plan of Pembroke Castle.
18. Raglan Castle.

CHAPTER 4

CHAPTER 6

CHAPTER 8

Pembroke Castle, Pembrokeshire.

Aberystwyth Castle, Ceredigion.

INTRODUCTION

Wales is littered with the relics of war, including Roman forts, medieval castles, single round towers and the coastal forts of the eighteenth and nineteenth centuries that replaced castles as the main method of defence. The remains of the castles of the eleventh and twelfth centuries are still with us and are a major part of the history of Wales. These magnificent structures, which were built to withstand a frontal attack and to subdue the local inhabitants, have withstood the ravages of time and, thankfully, have been restored for the nation. Castles became strongholds and the seats of local lords and barons. A castle was not only a base for a garrison, but also a formidable defence against an attacker, boasting massive ramparts, impregnable walls and lofty towers for its defenders.

The concept of the eighteenth-century forts was rather different. These strongholds' main purpose was housing powerful guns, usually encased in thick walls. Their sole purpose was defence against a sea-borne invasion.

The twentieth century introduced new modes of defences, especially during the two world wars. More 'moderate' forms of defence included concrete or brick pillboxes, barbed wire, ditches and gun emplacements.

Airfields were introduced during the First World War, but it was during the Second World War that they were fully utilised. In Wales, twenty-two airfields had concrete and tarmac runways, which are still visible today. Although others had only a grass landing area, some of the buildings are still intact. The airfields had unique infrastructures, such as the hangars, concrete and brick watchtowers (or control towers) and half-buried command/operational centres. Most of these structures are disappearing; in a short time they will be lost to future generations. However, some have been preserved for the future, such as the impressive hangars at the flying-boat station at Pembroke Dock and the unique control tower at Carew airfield, both in Pembrokeshire. At the time of writing, only one of the wartime airfields is still operational.

During the period between 1946 and 1980, a new type of structure came into being – the concrete bunker capable of withstanding a nuclear blast. Regional headquarters (or control centres) were rotor bunkers with radar installation. Rather smaller Royal Observer Corp underground posts were also located throughout the country. Most of these structures are not noticeable to the public; they are usually hidden by overgrowth or situated in deserted locations. Today, all are surplus to requirements and some are even up for sale.

All the structures remind us of the ability of the Welsh people to survive against all odds. The relics of the twentieth century do not have the sheer majesty of the castles of Edward I, but they are part of that unique and special history and should be preserved for future generations.

1

EARLY FORTIFICATIONS

The earliest types of fortification in Wales were the hillforts built during the Iron Age. Settlements were often targets for robbers and even jealous neighbours, and communities had realised that the best method of protecting their interests, families, homes and livestock was to build the homestead on a hill surrounded with a wooden (or brush) hedge. Such structures provided protection against wild animals and unwanted intruders.

The hillforts in Wales are usually classed as 'medium' or 'large'. The medium forts covered an area of about three acres while the large ones enclosed approximately fifteen acres.

Forts, or defended areas, consisted of an area enclosed within a single stone wall or a double rampart. Some larger settlements had stone buildings rather than the turf huts that were most common. The majority of the forts built in Wales were situated on hills overlooking fertile river valleys, although some were built on the coast, with fishing as the main food source. Good examples of coastal forts are on Conwy Mountain and Pen-y-Dorian on the Great Orme in Llandudno, some four miles apart. Distances between hillforts varied, but they were usually over five miles apart. Many believe that considerable trading took place between the various settlements. In some parts of Wales there are a cluster of such hillforts, indicating close trading.

Forts usually occupied hilltops, some on the edge of a spur or a ridge. The remains of some have been found on cliff tops, occupying high grounds that could be easily protected.

Other settlements were built in valleys, near water and fertile land for animals and crops. A series of small forts or look-out towers were built on nearby hills or mountains, providing an all-round view of the valley and its approaches; a good example is Foel Fenlli above the Clwyd Valley. Another example is Tre Ceiri in North Wales, which had at least 150 huts and was used until the end of the fourth century.

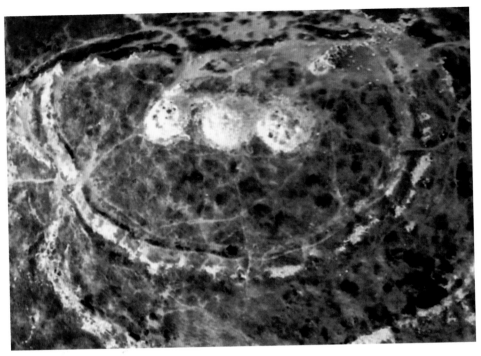

1. The remains of Foel Drygarn hillfort.

With the establishment of an aristocratic style of society in various areas, a headperson was nominated as a chieftain of a settlement. Communities became larger and wealthier, rivalry emerged between settlements, and fear played a part in their relationships between groups. By the end of the first century BC, the Welsh population had formed distinct tribal groups. Eventually some chieftains' powers increased and they were able to become princes of large areas.

Farming was the main occupation of the settlements. It provided food for the inhabitants and surplus food for trading. Some settlements were renowned for manufacturing clay pots and producing iron tools and arms. Initially the inhabitants were more concerned about protecting their settlements from wild animals than attacks from other communities, but as settlements became wealthier, their priorities changed.

In the early hillforts, wood was the most common material used, as the majority of Wales was woodland. Stone dwelling places and walls did not appear in Wales until around 500 BC.

Favourite positions for coastal forts were on ridges that ran seaward; a stone wall could be built across the neck of the ridge. Good examples of such forts can be found along the Pembrokeshire coastal path. Most were of the medium type. Large forts were common in the Black Mountains and the

Berwyn Mountains. Others were erected in areas where copper was mined; a well-preserved example is Oswestry Old Fort, with its rampart walls and sheer ditches. There is evidence that within its walls there were at least 150 huts, plus a large roundhouse with a thick stone wall and turf and a thatch roof.

ROMAN FORTS

During the Roman occupation of Wales there was a sharp increase in the building of forts, watchtowers and walled towns. Sadly, as the majority of these fortifications were built of wood, none are left today.

The second Roman invasion of Britain took place in AD 47 and expansion across Wales was gradual. A control centre was established at Shrewsbury and the invaders eventually proceeded along the Llangollen Valley. Initially all the Roman forts were built on the Welsh border, with bases at Gloucester and Chester.

By AD 79, a large number of the Welsh tribes had been forcibly defeated and subdued. The Roman governor Agricola built at least twenty forts throughout Wales, manned by around 10,000 troops. The great walled towns of Gloucester, Wroxeter and Chester controlled the main access to Wales, therefore keeping a tight grip on the tribes that threatened the Roman way of life.

A large fortress was built at Caerleon (Isca) to control the coastal plain between Cardiff and Carmarthen Bay. Another fortress was built at Caernarfon that, together with Chester, controlled the North Wales coastal area. Only the south-western part of the country did not have any Roman forts.

Some fifty years after the Welsh nation had been subdued, there were still fourteen forts in the country. From AD 284–305, a number of civilian settlements emerged alongside the forts at Carmarthen and Caerwent.

As a number of Roman villas rich in gold, silver and other fineries had been built, the Irish king Niall saw an opportunity to raid the coastal areas around Wales. To deter these raids, several smaller forts were built and together with the existing forts – re-garrisoned with several hundred troops – they put a temporary end to the raids. A good example was the posting of nearly 260 soldiers to the old fort at Dinorben.

During the fourth century, new coastal forts were built at Holyhead, Caernarfon and Cardiff. The large legionary fort at Chester was reinforced with stone walls.

Between AD 365 and 367, raids on the Welsh coast increased and security became a great concern for the governor. At the same time, the Continental borders of the empire were also being attacked.

In AD 368, four units of legionaries arrived in Wales to drive out the invaders and the local chieftains were persuaded to join the fight. By this time the Roman

2. A stone Roman watchtower at Caerleon.

Empire was in turmoil, with threat of invasions from every corner of its empire as well as the usual unrest within the Roman establishment itself. Various governors and generals were jockeying for political power and leadership. In Wales, a number of prospective local leaders waited for the Romans to depart.

In AD 411, Emperor Honorius removed the Roman legion from Wales and advised the towns and settlements to arrange their own defence. In the Romanised areas of Wales, the civic authority in place was modelled on the Romans'. This helped with the formation of a defence force, based on the Roman legions, to protect the walled towns that existed. Other areas returned in many ways to a tribal system.

THE DARK AGES

The period that is known as the Dark Ages, which lasted some 500 years, began when the Romans left Wales. The country was left in a vacuum. Historians have been baffled by the events of this period. Many believe that the Romanised areas remained the same for some time, based on the Roman model, although the Welsh people eventually reclaimed some of their culture.

The forts, roads and town walls remained. However, stone and wooden material from Roman aqueducts were used to build houses and so on.

Elsewhere in Britain, the Saxon burgh (or tun) – a timbered wall and ditch – was adopted around settlements for defence. In Wales the situation was rather different; the Welsh adopted a combination of burgh, Iron Age hillfort and Roman fort.

The next interesting construction took place in the eighth century, during the time of King Offa. The Anglo-Saxon king had obtained a foothold in most of England and had pushed westward into the Celtic part of the country, but failed to get beyond the River Wye. The reason was that the Welsh tribes amalgamated and won a great victory over the invaders in around AD 620–30.

The Kingdom of Mercia under Offa bordered Wales. In AD 760 there was large battle at Hereford, where Offa had built a wooden border fortress. The Welsh tribes were a thorn in Offa's side as they raided Mercia frequently, stealing their cattle. To teach the Welsh a lesson, his army invaded Dyfed three times, in AD 778, 784 and 796.

These raids did not solve the problem, and in 790 he built a dyke marking the boundary between Mercia and Wales. The dyke, known in Welsh as 'Clawdd Offa', ran for 150 miles from the mouth of the River Wye in the south to the River Dee in the north. It is the longest monument in Britain, consisting of earth ramparts on the English side and a deep ditch on the Welsh. In certain parts, Offa made use of the natural features, including hills, mountains and rivers. Some historians believe that wooden fortresses and watchtowers were built along the dyke.

The next episode in the history of Wales was the constant threat from the sea by Scandinavian attackers. It was the Danish kings in 851 that posed the biggest threat, by attacking the undefended coastal areas of West Wales. The Welsh tribes eventually joined forces and chose one leader, Rhodri Mawr (Rhodri the Great), who not only defeated the Danes but brought unity to a divided nation and began building motte-and-bailey fortifications around Wales. After his death, the nation reverted back to three regions, each with its own leader.

2

THE CASTLE-BUILDING ERA

The term 'castle' conjures up various images, from fairytale structures to sinister and mystical buildings housing sorcerers and villains. Some are linked to historical exploits of kings and brave knights, while others are linked with treachery and cruelty. A great number of the castles are associated with Welsh legends, including the exploits recorded in the *Mabinogion*.

There are at least 204 castles in Wales; the sites of some date back to pre-Roman times. Today the term 'castle' is used loosely, as some are just a motte and bailey, a single tower, or even a fortified family home.

The motte-and-bailey design was one of the earliest forms of castle fortification. A motte is either an artificial or natural mound of earth, or even a hill where a castle or a single tower was built. There are several such examples of mounds in Wales, which had a small stone wall or high hedge or timber walls. Single towers were a common and cheap type of fortification, usually manned by a few knights and their servants. Often these towers extended from the main castles and were part of the outer defence. Several villages were built in close proximity to the towers, to take advantage of the protection provided by the men-at-arms. Although the towers are often referred to locally as castles, they should actually be classed as watchtowers.

Some fortified family homes built by wealthy individuals and landowners are often referred to as castles, but are in fact only ordinary homes and estates that have been fortified by their owners. During the Victorian period, several buildings were built with castle frontage and round towers; these became to be known as 'follies'.

All the castles referred to as such in this book are true castles – either motte and bailey, or with stone walls, round or square towers, turrets, battlements, great halls and gatehouses. Some have a bailey bridge and moat.

Medieval castles were formidable fortifications and were often only manned by a small garrison of men at arms, sometimes a knight and a large force of archers,

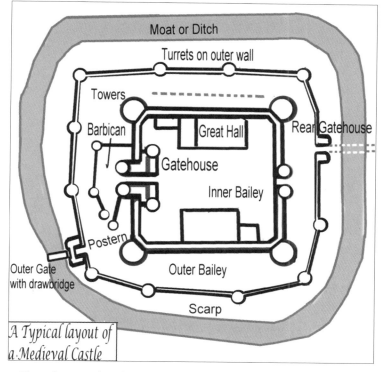

Moat or Ditch

Turrets on outer wall

Towers

Barbican

Great Hall

Rear Gatehouse

Gatehouse

Inner Bailey

Postern

Outer Gate
with drawbridge

Outer Bailey

Scarp

A Typical layout of a Medieval Castle

3. Plan of a typical medieval castle.

Ben Phillips 2009

4. Sketch of an early motte-and-bailey fortification.

5. A castle walkway at Pembroke Castle.

who were the main defenders on castle walls and turrets. There are a number of instances where a small castle garrison held out against an overwhelming attacking force.

The true castle-building period was between the eleventh and the mid-fifteenth centuries. When the Normans invade Britain they brought with them not only their way of life and their ruling structures, but also their method of castle construction. The basic design remained the same for centuries.

The Normans' first march into Wales was in 1067, when a Norman knight, William FitzOsbern, made a limited invasion into South Wales. To consolidate his position, he built a number of castles. During the reigns of William II and Henry I, further attempts were made to subdue the Welsh by building castles and towers in the country. A great number of these fortified timber strongholds were strengthened with stone walls and keeps. It was soon realised that the Norman skills in warfare and castle-building were too much for the lightly armed Welsh tribes. Soon villages were built near the castles, as they provided protection for the inhabitants. As a result, more English and Norman inhabitants moved into the protected areas of Pembrokeshire and Glamorgan. Perhaps one of the most important early castles in Wales was at Pembroke, overlooking the estuary of Milford Haven, which had become an important sheltered inlet in West Wales.

With the death of Henry I in 1135, England was involved in a bitter civil war between the followers of Stephen and Matilda, which gave the Welsh population, under the leadership of Owain Gwynedd in the north, an opportunity to drive the Normans out of the country. In South Wales, Rhys ap Gruffydd drove most of the Normans out, with the exception of Pembrokeshire. As a result, the Welsh gained several of the invaders' castles and strongholds and were able to unite as one nation. For the next twenty years, the Welsh nation was able to put its stamp on the castles.

In 1176, Cardigan Castle became the venue of the first gatherings of the bards organised by Rhys ap Gryffudd. This set the standard for all future eisteddfods.

Another great Welsh leader was Llywelyn ap Iorwerth, or Llywelyn the Great. He began as leader of Gwynedd in the north, but soon extended his influence to the rest of Wales. When Llywelyn died in 1240, Wales ended up with the same problems England had experienced with royal succession.

The next great leader was no doubt Llywelyn the Great's grandson, Llywelyn ap Gruffydd, who styled himself as the Prince of Wales. At the Treaty of Montgomery, Henry III was compelled to recognise Llywelyn as the Prince of Wales.

When Edward I succeeded to the throne in 1272, the situation in Wales changed completely. The King was not prepared to have two unruly independent states – Wales and Scotland – on his borders. Llywelyn, operating out of his castles in Wales, underestimated Edward's motives and determination. After a series of battles, Llywelyn's army was defeated and had to retreat into the hills as Edward had occupied most of the coastal area and had seized the castles. New, large English castles were built at Flint, Rhuddlan, Aberystwyth and Builth, emphasising Edward's power and threatening the Welsh into submission. These castles were manned by several hundred knights and soldiers and, with the exception of Builth, could be easily supplied from the sea or river.

Edward was adamant that he would have the best and most formidable strongholds ever built in the British Isles. Special masons and workers were recruited from Savoy, under the leadership of perhaps the best castle architect in Europe, Master James of St George. Master James was involved in the construction of twelve of the castles in Wales. He perfected the symmetrical castle design, with the 'walls within walls' that are characteristic of his work. These designs became the blueprint for all castles built thereafter.

With Edward's army operating out of the new and captured castles, Llywelyn's supporters began to dwindle. After a series of defeats, the Prince of Wales returned north in 1282. On the way, a group of English soldiers attacked his army and Llywelyn was killed in the battle.

Within five years the Welsh had regrouped under Llywelyn's brother Dafydd, who had previously backed Edward, but felt that he had not been rewarded by the English king for his services. Dafydd was betrayed, captured, and put to death in Shrewsbury in 1283.

Dafydd's short campaign was followed by another round of castle building, notably at Conwy, Caernarfon and Harlech. The Welsh aristocracy was totally destroyed and an English system of administration was put in place, including the English method of taxation, which infuriated not only the Welsh but also the English settlers.

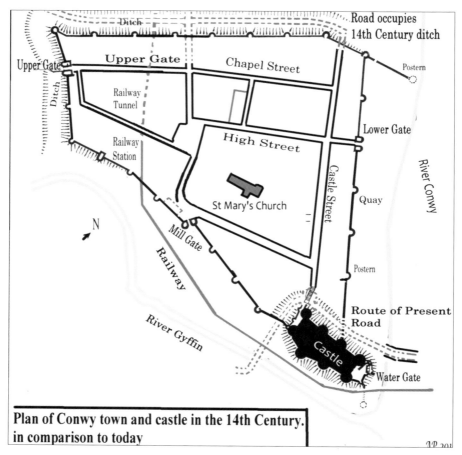

6. Layout map of Conwy Castle and town in the fourteenth century.

Another short rebellion under Prince Madog took place in 1294, which necessitated Edward sending a force of 30,000 men led by the Earl of Warwick into North Wales. Resistance to this massive force was soon subdued. To keep an eye on the area, a castle was built at Beaumaris in Anglesey.

Edward's large castle-building programme and his military expedition into Wales emptied his treasury. To avoid bankruptcy, he raised taxes for the people of both Wales and England and castle-building came to an abrupt end, although some castles were modified and redeveloped to Master James of St George's standard.

For the next ninety years, Wales settled down to a period of uneasy peace, with an occasional skirmish instantly quelled by the garrisons based in the various castles.

The next uprising to shatter the peace was that of Owain Glyndwr in 1400. Glyndwr took advantage of the Epiphany Rising in England and Henry IV's subsequent preoccupation with hanging on to his crown. The rebellion travelled through Wales very quickly, and the first castle to be destroyed was Ruthin. Henry sent an army to put down the rebellion but was beaten back by adverse weather. Glyndwr continued to advance through Wales, putting English settlements to the torch and capturing some of Edward's mighty castles. A French fleet in the Irish Sea bombarded and destroyed the English garrisons on the coast at Aberystwyth and Criccieth, while in the east Glyndwr's army marched as far as Worcester.

For some strange reason, the rebellion came to an abrupt end in 1410, having lost its momentum. Owain Glyndwr went into hiding and disappeared from the scene. The castles taken by Glyndwr were retaken with very little resistance. The Welsh were renowned for capturing castles and then being unable to hold them. There was hardly a castle in Wales not attacked or captured by Owain Glyndwr's army.

For the next ten years, the castles of Wales fell into disrepair; those damaged in the rebellion of Owain Glyndwr were not restored.

Eventually, after years of neglect, certain gentry saw that war clouds involving the houses of York and Lancaster were forming. Great effort was put into completing the last great castle of Wales at Raglan. This castle, with typical multi-angular towers, was built by a Tudor architect.

The Wars of the Roses played a significant part in the nation's history, since they put on the throne a Welshman born at Pembroke Castle. Henry Tudor had a good claim to the English throne and was determined to heal the rift between the House of Lancaster and York. With a small force, he landed at Milford Haven in 1485 and was joined by Rhys ap Thomas, a powerful lord of South Wales, who pledged his full support. Henry's force marched through Wales and was joined by thousands of followers and culminated in the defeat of Richard III on Bosworth Field. Henry Tudor became Henry VII – a Welshman on an English throne.

Wales was fortunate to have years of peace under the Tudors, and castle-building had come to an end. The established ones were occupied by various individuals who had been loyal to the monarchy, but they were expected to keep small garrisons to keep the peace and to provide men for any future conflicts.

Today, thanks to organisations like Cadw, Welsh flags fly from most of the castles of Wales.

A List of the Major Castles in Wales

The following alphabetical list includes all structures with stone walls, round towers, great halls, round or square towers, keeps or gatehouses. Some have bailey bridges and a moat.

7. Map showing the main castles of Wales.

ABERYSTWYTH CASTLE, CEREDIGION

A Norman, Lord Gilbert de Clare, built the first castle in Aberystwyth, at Llanfarian in the Ystwydd Valley, some two miles south of the present site. The original castle was a modest construction of timber and stone that was attacked and rebuilt frequently.

In 1171, Cardiganshire was given by Henry II to Rhys ap Gruffydd, a self-proclaimed ruler of South Wales. As a result of a family feud following his death, one of his sons, Maelgwyn, seized the territory. In 1207, fearing an attack by Llywelyn the Great, Maelgwyn destroyed the castle, but it was later rebuilt. The family dispute regarding the castle's ownership continued for several years.

In 1215, Llywelyn the Great captured Cardigan Castle and eventually took possession of the castle at Aberystwyth. For the next sixteen years the site was captured and recaptured several times.

In the latter part of the thirteenth century, Edward I built the castle on its present site. Aberystwyth Castle, overlooking Cardigan Bay, became one of the strongest defences on the west coast.

In 1404, Owain Glyndwr captured the town and the castle, but it was retaken by Prince Henry's forces three years later, then again by Glyndwr's army, and yet again by the English.

During the Tudor period, the castles of Wales and their inhabitants enjoyed a time of peace and stability.

The next military phase for the castle was during the First English Civil War (1642–46). As with other Welsh castles, the owners supported the Royalist cause until forced to surrender to the Parliamentarian Colonel Rice Powell after a siege in 1646. For supporting the Royalists, Oliver Cromwell ordered the castle to be demolished in 1647.

BEAUMARIS CASTLE, ANGLESEY

After the death of Llywelyn, Prince of Wales, many of his army escaped to Anglesey, where they became a lingering thorn in Edward's side. Both Caernarfon and Conwy castles guarded the entrances to the hinterland, but there was still a gap in total defence, especially when Prince Madoc's forces captured and partially burned Caernarfon Castle. To strengthen his hold on the Menai Straits, Edward commissioned a new castle to be built at Beaumaris in 1295; this was the last of Edward's great castles in North Wales.

The site chosen was unusual as it was low and flat, which Master James of

St George made good use of. The inner bailey was protected by high, 15-foot-thick walls and six awesome towers, two being half towers. Entrance to the inner bailey was through two mighty fortified gatehouses. The castle's outer bailey was protected by a series of twelve small towers with two well-defended outer gatehouses, built around 1315. A channel, guarded by the south gateway, was dug to join the moat to the sea. The castle was capable of maintaining a large garrison, but became an expensive 'white elephant' as its defences were never tested.

During the Civil War, the castle was garrisoned by Thomas, Lord Bulkeley, who surrendered to Parliamentarian forces in 1646 after the Royalists were defeated in a nearby battle. As the castle was not involved in any further action, it was saved from demolition.

BRECON CASTLE, BRECONSHIRE

Bernard de Mewmarch built a simple motte and bailey after he captured the kingdom of Brycheiniog from the Welsh princes. Most of the walls of the castle were built with stones from the nearby old Roman camp of Caer Bannan. As a relative of William the Conqueror, he was granted the title of Lord of Brecon. The title made him a number of enemies among the English as well as the Welsh. Several upgrades were made to the fortification over the years. In the twelfth century, a polygonal shell on the motte was added, with a hall. The round tower was added in the thirteenth century and another semi-octagonal tower in early fourteenth century.

Brecon Castle, under Sir Thomas Berkley's ownership, became a frequent target during Owain Glyndwr's campaign. In 1404, the lords of Audley and Warwick were put in charge of defending the castle and the King provided a hundred men-at-arms and eleven mounted archers.

Ownership of the castle changed hands frequently during its history. In 1215 it was attacked and captured. It was attacked again in 1231 and 1233, captured in 1264, and recaptured a year later. Further attacks in 1273 and 1403 (the latter by Owain Glyndwr's army) caused substantial damage. A short period of peace followed the marriage of Henry Tudor and Elizabeth, the daughter of Edward IV, which united the houses of Lancaster and York.

During the reign of Richard III, the Duke of Buckingham was the Lord of Brecon and Morton. The Bishop of Ely was imprisoned in the castle tower. By this time, the importance of Brecon Castle had diminished and it began falling into ruins.

CAERNARFON CASTLE, GWYNEDD

One of the best-preserved strongholds in Wales, Caernarfon Castle was built by Edward I to subdue the Welsh and control their country.

After a series of battles with Llywelyn's army, Edward occupied most of the coastal area of North Wales and soon seized the Welsh castles. He built new ones and fortified the rest. They were manned by several hundred knights and soldiers and could be easily supplied from the sea or river.

Caernarfon was designed and built by Master James of St George and it became renowned throughout Europe as the ultimate in military architecture and engineering.

The castle was built on a small peninsula near the entrance of the Menai Straits, on the site of an earlier motte-and-bailey castle of the late twelfth century. Construction of Edward's castle began in 1283, with workers and material brought in from England by sea. To ensure complete safety during the construction, town walls and a fortified dock were built simultaneously, putting great pressure on the workforce. Within eight years, the whole external southern section, including the Eagle Tower, the North-East Tower and the town wall, were nearly complete. Confident in the strength and safety of the castle, Edward and Queen Eleanor stayed there, in temporary accommodation, in 1283.

8. Caernarfon Castle.

By 1287, most of the castle's infrastructure was completed, although detail-finishing and alterations continued for some years.

By 1292, £12,000 had been spent on the castle. Total expendidture was almost £50,000 over a fifty-year period. Only Conwy Castle cost more.

Also involved with its building was Walter of Hereford, another distinguished castle builder of the period, who took over the construction in 1294.

In 1294, Prince Madoc's forces gained entrance through an uncompleted section of the castle wall, seizing and burning most of the timber structure before being defeated. As the result, priority was given to starting the defence on the northern side, the town side and water side.

Between 1295 and 1301, the north-end defences – the town wall, its towers and the King's Gate – were completed. Further strengthening of the defences occurred between 1304 and 1305, and between 1309 and 1327.

The castle consisted of thirteen towers of various designs and several entrances, of which the largest is the distinguished archway of the King's Gate. Two large towers, a drawbridge and at least five doors and six portcullises defended the gateway. Originally there was a plan to build a moat, but it did not materialise. It is worth noting that the strong construction of the Eagle Tower resembles a keep with its own portcullises and postern with four turrets. The other exceptional tower is the Queen's Tower, next to the great banqueting hall. The other towers were the Chamberlain Tower, Black Tower and the Cistern Tower, leading to the Queen's Gate. North of the gate there is the North-East Tower and the Granary Tower. The Eagle, Queen, Chamberlain and Black towers were all used for accommodation. All the castle's walls have walkways with battlements and the towers and gatehouses have ample arrow slits for defence.

In 1401, 1403 and 1404 Owain Glyndwr's forces attacked and besieged the castle without any success.

With the accession of the Tudors, Wales enjoyed peace and prosperity until the English Civil War. As with most Welsh castles, it was held by Royalist forces until 1644, when Parliamentarians under Captain Sweeney captured it. Within a year, the castle and the town were recaptured by Royalists under the command of Lord Byron; in 1646 it was again lost to Parliamentarian forces.

During the reign of Charles II the castle was earmarked for demolition, but the order was never carried out.

In 1908, the castle was taken over by the Crown and urgent restoration began to repair the damage of wars and neglect.

Caernarfon Castle's recent claim to fame was in 1969, when it was the venue for the investiture of Prince Charles, Prince of Wales.

CAERPHILLY CASTLE, GLAMORGAN

This is the largest castle in Wales, for it covers an area of nearly 30 acres. It was the first concentric castle in Britain. Work on the castle was begun in 1268 by Gilbert de Clare, Earl of Gloucester and Lord of Glamorgan, in response to the advances made by Llywelyn, Prince of Wales, in South Wales. The castle was built near the site of a Roman fortification. When the Romans left Britain in AD 410, a Welsh chieftain used the site.

The original de Clare castle and a later one were attacked and destroyed by Llywelyn's forces. Construction of the present castle began on 1 June 1271 and it took ten years to complete. Its construction made use of the combination of both land and water, especially using the two lakes as a defence barrier. It had three well-protected wards, with seven fortified gatehouses within the castle itself and on the outer curtain wall, which formed a well-defended barbican. The castle had a fairly square inner bailey with four large towers and two large gatehouses. The gatehouses and towers were situated some distance from the court and the walls were separated by at least thirty portcullis doorways. The castle's first test of strength came when, in 1321, the barons attacked Glamorgan and captured Caerphilly Castle. Edward II came to the defence of his supporter Hugh le Despenser, subdued the revolt, and recaptured the castle.

9. Caerphilly Castle.

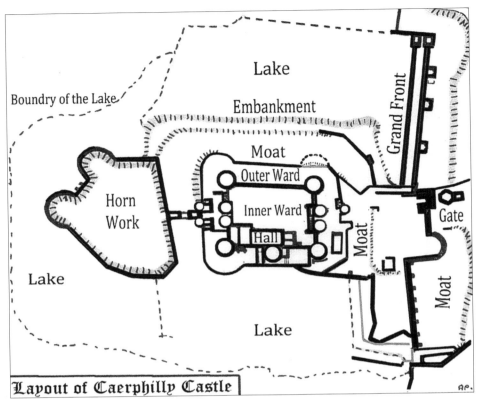

10. Layout plan of Caerphilly Castle.

In 1326, Queen Isabella returned to Britain with a group of exiled noblemen, determined to seek out their enemies. The King fled, once again seeking support from Hugh le Despenser at Caerphilly Castle.

In 1326–27, Queen Isabella's army besieged the castle and after a long siege the occupants surrendered after favourable peace terms were worked out. The King was captured near Llantrisant and taken to Berkeley Castle, while Despenser was caught and executed at Bristol.

The castle was captured and held by Owain Glyndwr for a brief period.

By 1536, the castle's importance had diminished and it fell into neglect and disrepair.

During the Civil War of 1642, the castle, then under Royalist control, was fortified with cannons and muskets. The north-western earthwork was expanded so that artillery could be embedded to defend the northern approach.

Caerphilly Castle's trademark is its half-demolished leaning tower. There are several accounts of how the tower came to be in this position. One account was that Queen Isabella's forces undermined the tower during the siege. Another said that it was damaged by an internal explosion. The most likely explanation is that the Parliamentarians tried to demolish the castle after the conclusion of the English Civil War.

CARDIFF CASTLE

This castle is situated west of the city centre on a site of former strongholds. The present castle dates back to around 1091, when Robert FitzHamon built an earth-and-wood fortress on the site of an earlier Welsh stronghold. It was a motte-and-bailey type, with a wooden tower built on the motte. After the Welsh revolts of 1183–84, the castle and settlement were badly damaged, but the castle was strengthened and the town fortified.

Robert 'the Consul' refortified the castle with the building of a 40-foot stone keep on the motte, surrounded by a moat. He also improved the town's defences.

The castle was handed to Gilbert de Clare, who strengthened the castle and the town defences further, fearing attacks from Llywelyn's advances in South Wales. He rebuilt the curtain wall and constructed the Black Tower on the south gatehouse. It is believed that the Black Tower was the prison of Robert, Duke of Normandy, in 1106.

The castle was further strengthened, especially after Owain Glyndwr's attack in 1404, which also burned the town. The castle walls were rebuilt, as well as an octagonal tower and additional domestic buildings.

When Henry Tudor gained the English throne, Cardiff Castle was given to Jasper Tudor, his uncle, who continued to restore and rebuild the castle.

By the time of the English Civil War, the castle had been handed down to William Herbert, a staunch Royalist, but when the King's army was defeated by Parliamentarians at St Fagan's, the castle's garrison surrendered.

In 1766, the castle was owned by the Bute family, who made several improvements to the castle, not so much for defence but rather on the living side. In 1800 a prominent mansion was built on the castle grounds, utilising a lot of the stones from the castle itself.

CAREW CASTLE, PEMBROKESHIRE

This is another castle built by Rhys, Prince of South Wales, but it was taken over by the Normans in 1095 when Gerald de Windsor married Nest, the daughter of the Welsh prince. Initially, the castle consisted of motte and bailey with a gatehouse.

Considerable rebuilding was done during the Tudor period, with the building of four large towers. In the fifteenth century, a descendant of Gerald and Nest, Sir Edmund Carew, mortgaged the castle to Sir Rhys ap Thomas, who eventually marched with Henry to Bosworth and defeated Richard III.

More lavish alteration was done by another wealthy owner, Sir John Perrott, and the castle became renowned for its sumptuous state apartments and festivities, as well as for being an important strategic fortification.

The next military conflict to involve Carew Castle was the English Civil War. The Royalists went to great lengths to adapt the castle to the new mode of warfare by enlarging the arrow slits in the bastions for muskets and hand-held cannons.

All the work was in vain, as in 1642, after the fall of Tenby Castle, the occupants surrendered.

CARMARTHEN CASTLE, CARMARTHENSHIRE

The town of Carmarthen has a long history, going back to the Roman period, when the settlement was called Moridunum. During the Dark Ages it was associated with the wizard Merlin.

Today, the twelfth-century castle is obscured by modern buildings built in the castle area. The initial motte and bailey was built in around 1105, but most of it was destroyed in an attack in 1215. It was rebuilt in 1223 with stone towers and strengthened walls. A grand gatehouse and smaller round tower were added in the fourteenth century. The castle was frequently used by the Welsh princes and became a target of the English forces.

Under English ownership, the castle was captured by Owain Glyndwr's forces in 1403. They lost it to the English and captured it again in 1405.

The Tudor era brought a period of peace to the inhabitants and owners.

During the English Civil War, Carmarthen Castle changed hands several times between the Royalists and the Parliamentarians. Each time a siege or an attack took place, the castle sustained considerable damage. It was during the conflict that the Royalists constructed an earthwork for additional protection against siege guns, part of which can still be seen to the west of the town. After the defeat of the Royalists, the Parliamentarians dismantled the castle.

CARREG CENNEN CASTLE, CARMARTHENSHIRE

This castle was built on a former Roman site situated on a rocky crag overlooking the valley of the Afon Cennen. Two towers guard the only way to the castle, while a strong wall with a sheer drop of 300 feet protects the other sides.

The castle was one of the most important fortifications in Welsh history, for it was located in the centre of Is Cennen, part of the kingdom of Deheubarth, whose royal residence was at Dinefwr. The site was of great strategic importance, as it had a clear view over the valley and surrounding area. The castle was constructed in three stages between the late thirteenth and early fourteenth centuries. The initial phase was the towered inner ward – the nucleus of the castle, with a chapel and gatehouse. It seems only a small part of the walls dating from the Welsh period were utilised. Next to be built was the barbican and the outer wall. The approach to the castle was along a fairly narrow ridge, a barbican ramp, and a middle drawbridge, which lead through a heavily defended gatehouse to the inner ward. Another interesting feature of the castle was a long passage leading to a cave underneath the structure.

The original Welsh stronghold fell to the overwhelming forces of Edward I, which had advanced up the River Towy from Kidwelly. The castle was briefly recaptured during Edward's second offensive in 1282. John Gifford, who was in charge of Llandovery Castle, was also put in charge of Carreg Cennen. Over the next few years, John Gifford made extensive repairs to the castle. In 1286, the castle was retaken by the Welsh during Rhys ap Maredudd's uprising, but it was recaptured and came under the custody of the Earl of Hereford. Gifford returned to the castle, which he held for the next sixteen years.

Hugh le Despenser became the most influential and powerful baron in South Wales, and during his bid to take over the Gower, Gifford, together with other Marcher Lords, opposed him. Edward sent an army to quench the rebellion, Gifford was executed for treason and Depenser was given Carreg Cennen Castle.

For his support of Edward's actions, Despenser was executed by the order of Queen Isabella in 1325 and the castle changed hand several times thereafter.

On the accession of Henry Bolingbroke as Henry IV, the castle became Crown property. At the time, the castle was regarded as impregnable. It was attacked by Owain Glyndwr in 1403, but he failed to capture it.

During the Wars of the Roses, Gruffydd ap Nicholas, a supporter of the House of Lancaster, garrisoned the castle. After the battle of Mortimer Cross, Gryffydd's sons took refuge at the castle, but after a short siege in 1462 Sir Richard Herbert of Raglan Castle persuaded the occupants to surrender. Later that year, it was decided to demolish the castle and make it inhabitable.

Henry VII gave the castle to Sir Rhys ap Thomas for his service to the Crown. Until the early nineteenth century, the castle belonged to the Vaughan family of Golden Grove, who bequeathed it to the earls of Cawdor.

CHEPSTOW CASTLE, MONMOUTHSHIRE

The original Chepstow Castle was founded by a Norman lord, William FitzOsbern, who was made the Earl of Hereford and was eager to extend his boundaries westward into Wales. The site was of great strategic importance, for it controlled the main route over the River Wye and commanded the harbour. The castle construction began around 1067 as the Normans pushed westward. It occupies a long, narrow ridge on the southern bank of the River Wye and is separated from the town by a deep gully known as 'the Dingle'. In the middle of the castle is the Great Tower. On the west side is the upper bailey, with a barbican and a gatehouse. On the eastern side are the middle bailey and the lower bailey with its great hall, a smaller hall, Marten's Tower, the great gatehouse and another barbican. The domestic buildings were added towards the end of the thirteenth century.

In 1650, the south-facing curtain wall was strengthened to house cannons. Over the years, ownership of the castle changed several times.

The first recorded attack on the castle was by Hywel ap Iorwerth in 1173.

In 1176, the castle was the home of Isabella de Clare, the heir to the estate. Because of her importance, a royal constable, a chaplain, domestic staff, three watchmen, ten men-at-arms, ten archers plus the castle garrison of another fifteen men-at-arms protected her. Isabella eventually married William Marshall in 1189, and the castle defences were updated. The rebuilding was continued by their sons, who inherited the castle. From 1270, the rebuilding went on for about thirty years, except for a five-year period when the town walls were being built.

The castle was inherited by John Bigod, but on his death, all his lands, including the castle, were bequeathed to the Crown to pay his debts.

Edward II appointed royal constables to oversee the castles; one was the hated Hugh le Despenser, who carried out some repair work on the infrastructure. Queen Isabella's forces captured the castle in 1326.

Thomas de Brotherton took ownership and eventually, in 1399, it was in the possession of Thomas Mowbray, Duke of Norfolk.

Throughout Owain Glyndwr's uprising, the castle was only manned by twenty men-at-arms and sixty archers.

In 1405, Thomas Mowbray was executed for treason and the castle was taken over by William Herbert, who was Lord of Raglan and the Earl of Pembroke.

For the next period, all construction and restoration concentrated on the domestic section, while the defences were neglected. As expected, the family were ardent Royalists who, during the early stages of the English Civil War, held the castle for the cause. By 1643, the Parliamentarians had made significant gains

11. Aerial view of Chepstow Castle. (*Cadw*)

throughout the country. Fearing a massive defeat, the family abandoned the castle and town in April. The King's army reoccupied the castle, but while the Parliamentarians prepared to besiege it, the Royalists attacked their stronghold at Monmouth. The Parliamentarians abandoned the siege to relieve Monmouth. By 1645, the Royalists were more or less beaten and Chepstow Castle fell to a token force. During the Second English Civil War, Sir Nicholas Kemeys and 120 men held out against Cromwell's forces. Eventually, the Parliamentarian artillery breached the walls and the occupants surrendered. Sir Nicholas was killed in the bombardment.

After the English Civil War, a garrison of Cromwell's army used the castle until 1660.

With the Restoration, Charles II appointed Lord Herbert, the son of William Herbert, as custodian. He kept a garrison at the castle. Chepstow Castle was used as a prison between 1660 and 1680.

In 1690, the Crown ordered the castle to be dismantled and its guns taken to defend Chester.

CHIRK CASTLE, DENBIGHSHIRE

Chirk Castle, or Castell y Waun as it is known in Welsh, is some six miles from Llangollen on the Welsh side of the border. The Welsh princes built a stronghold on the site in the eleventh century. As Edward's English army overwhelmed the area, a castle was constructed on the site in 1283 by one of Mortimer's Marcher Lords, Roger, who gained his appointment as a reward for defeating Llywelyn, Prince of Wales. The strengthening and rebuilding of the castle took place around 1310. The rebuilding involved a north front of about 250 feet, with a large round tower on each corner of the rectangular design. Half-towers were also built on the faces. The design of the battlements allowed two men to walk side by side. The main courtyard is entered via a lavish archway between two drum towers.

In 1593, the castle was bought by Sir Thomas Myddelton, but when his son Thomas, a Parliamentarian, arrived at Chirk, to his surprise the castle was occupied by Royalists.

During the English Civil War, Thomas switched his support to Charles I and in 1659 Cromwell's army besieged Chirk. It was not long before Parliamentarian guns breached the castle defences. In an effort to avoid total destruction of the castle, Sir Thomas gave the order to surrender. Most of the castle has survived, except one wall and its towers.

CILGERRAN CASTLE, PEMBROKESHIRE

This castle stands on a rock above the left bank of the River Teifi. The Normans only conquered West Wales in 1093, after the death of Rhys ap Tewdwr, the ruler of the Kingdom of Deheubarth. As the Normans advanced west, they built castles at Cardigan, Carmarthen and Pembroke to control their territory.

Gerald de Windsor, one of Henry I's Marcher Lords, built the present Cilgerran Castle on the site of Cenarth Bychan, a fortified settlement of Cadwgan of Powys.

During the reign of Henry II, Lord Rhys captured Cilgerran in 1165, a year after Cardigan Castle fell to his advance through West Wales.

In 1204, William Marshall, the Earl of Pembroke, captured Cilgerran Castle. During Llywelyn the Great's uprising, Cilgerran Castle and the whole of Pembrokeshire were recaptured by his army. In 1223, the castle changed ownership once again – this time it was taken by William Marshall's eldest son. It was during a period of peace that the castle was extensively rebuilt to make full use of its location. The castle did not play any significant part in Llywelyn's uprising, but a great victory was won by Llywelyn in a battle fought nearby.

The castle remained under the control of the Marshall family until the death of Anselm in 1245. The Cantelupes and the related Hastings family were the next owners of the castle, and occupied it until the end of the fourteenth century. Sadly, the new owners neglected the castle, and by 1275 most of the furnishings had been stolen and removed. By 1325, the structure was classed as a ruin and recommended for demolition.

After the defeat of an English force by the Spanish fleet in 1372, Edward III, concerned about an invasion, ordered the castle to be repaired and strengthened.

In 1405, Cilgerran Castle was attacked and captured by Owain Glyndwr's army and, once again, considerable damage was done to the infrastructure. During the Wars of the Roses, the castle ended up the property of the Tudors.

In the 1536 Act of Union, Henry VIII abolished the Marcher Lordships and the Vaughan family was granted rights to the castle, rights that lasted well into the seventeenth century.

The castle layout was typical of the designs at the time – a motte and bailey defended by a ditch. There were two large towers and a gatehouse, plus an outer ward guarded by a substantial ditch. One great advantage the castle had was the steep slopes that surrounded it on three sides.

COITY CASTLE, GLAMORGANSHIRE

The castle at Coity can be attributed to Payn de Turbeville, one of Robert FitzHamon's knights who occupied Glamorgan. However, the castle was built by one of Payn's relatives, Sir Gilbert de Turbevillle, who married a daughter of a Welsh lord of Avan at the beginning of the thirteenth century. By the fourteenth century, Turbeville's territories had been divided and towards the end of the century Coity Castle became the property of Sir William Gamage. During Owain Glyndwr's offensive in Glamorgan in 1403, the castle was besieged for a considerable time, causing great concern to Henry IV in London. The Gamage family remained owners of the castle until the end of the sixteenth century.

Parts of the castle, such as the curtain wall of the inner ward, date back to the twelfth century, while the rest is of thirteenth-century construction.

The original stronghold was a typical Norman fort in a style known as ring work, which included a circular embankment surrounded by a deep ditch and topped by timber.

The castle had a large outer ward and a round inner ward with a square keep. To strengthen its defence, a tower was built out of the curve of the southern wall. In the fourteenth century, considerable rebuilding took place, with a new eastern gatehouse in the inner ward curtain. The wall was increased by few feet and a middle gate was built south of the keep, linking both wards. Other improvements were made to the keep, the chapel and various domestic quarters. The castle's inner ward had a substantial moat circling it, but during Tudor times the moat was filled in.

CONWY CASTLE, CONWY

Another of Master James of St George's masterpieces in Wales was built between 1283 and 1285. The site was of strategic importance as it guarded and controlled movement up the river valley. Conwy Castle is rather unique, as it is not a concentric design (walls within walls) and all the relevant castle buildings are within a distinctive elongated shape. The building of Conwy Castle took only two years, while Caernarfon Castle took nearly forty. In 1285, 1,275 masters at arms and archers, as well as over 1,500 workers, garrisoned the castle. Work was finally completed in 1290, with the cost a staggering £2.5 million in today's terms. It was the most expensive project devised by Edward.

The castle was built on a rocky foundation on the side of the River Conwy. It was protected by the river on one side, a small brook on the other, and a steep rocky escarpment. The strong, impressive town wall – complete with twenty-one turret towers – acted as a protected outer ward. The castle was protected by a high curtain with eight large towers, each surmounted by round turrets. There were two barbicans and, within its walls, a large bow-shaped great hall. The castle had two entrances, one in the eastern barbican. The main entrance had a ramp leading to a drawbridge and the western barbican. There was a guarded gateway between the two towers, leading into the outer ward and the great hall and other domestic buildings. There were lavish staterooms built for the King and Queen – the King Chambers, the King's Hall, and a chapel protected by a middle gate in the entrance to the inner wards. In 1294, the castle was besieged for a number of days by Prince Madoc's forces and, according to some sources, Welsh bowmen perched on the rocky hill that was part of the castle defence, causing problems forthe defenders.

When the threat of uprisings diminishing, the castle's importance declined and it soon fell into neglect. Edward III's son, the Black Prince, inherited the Welsh lands, and with them most of the castles. In the mid-fourteenth century, urgent maintenance was made at Conwy Castle.

In 1401, Gwylyn and Rhys Tewdwr claimed the castle for their true prince, Owain Glyndwr. They overwhelmed the castle's garrison of seventy-five men. During the Wars of the Roses the castle was held by supporters of the House of York, but was not directly involved in the war.

The Tudor period brought peace to Wales and as a result Conwy, like other castles, fell into neglect. In 1628, Viscount Conway bought the castle for a mere £100.

12. Conwy Castle.

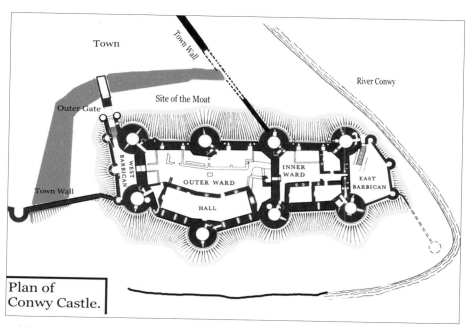

13. Plan of Conwy Castle.

14. Another view of
Conwy Castle.

During the English Civil War, John Williams, the Archbishop of York, who was a loyal supporter of the King, made urgent repairs to the castle. He also garrisoned the castle at his own expense – to the disgust of the then-governor of the castle, Sir John Owen. In 1646, Major-General Mytton and his Parliamentarian army besieged the castle, and within three months the town and the castle garrison had surrendered.

In 1660, Charles II handed the castle to the 3rd Earl of Conway, but, as the castle was in a bad condition, the earl began its demolition. All iron, lead and timber beams were removed, shipped to Ireland, and sold for a profit. In the nineteenth century, the local authority took responsibility for the castle and it was finally passed to the Government in 1953.

Today it has returned to Welsh control under Cadw.

CRICCIETH CASTLE, GWYNEDD

This castle is rather unique, as it consists of two different styles. It was originally a Welsh castle built in the early thirteenth century, at the time of Llywelyn the Great, on the crest of a headland flanked by two beaches. After the death of Llywelyn, Prince of Wales, in 1282 and during Edward's two campaigns in Wales, both Dolwyddelan and Criccieth castles were captured by the English. After Edward had established his authority over the Welsh in the area, a number of castles fell into disrepair. Criccieth Castle was in that category, so a large amount of money

15. Criccieth Castle. (*Cadw*)

was allocated to repair and strengthen the stronghold. The King employed William of Drogheda as master mason to refurbish Criccieth Castle, and many have noticed his influence on Master James's design for Harlech Castle. The reconstruction included a new inner ward built inside an irregular Welsh outer ward. As is common with the all-Welsh castles, it had three towers in the outer ward. Although the work began during the reign of Edward I, it continued well into the reign of Edward II. The outer ward was strengthened and a large, impressive twin-towered gatehouse was built in the new inner ward. Like Harlech, the gatehouse was heavy fortified and could be utilised as the castle keep. A new Edwardian tower was added to the Welsh towers that already existed on the outer walls. The gatehouse was strengthened and a defendable narrow passage was built between the two wards.

Criccieth Castle survived throughout the two revolts of 1288–94, but was cut off on the landward side. In 1359, the Prince of Wales appointed the first Welsh Constable to Criccieth, Sir Hywel ap Gruffydd. He remained there until his death in 1380. During Owain Glyndwr's uprising of 1400, Criccieth Castle was re-garrisoned by six men-at-arms and fifty archers. Throughout the conflict, Criccieth and Harlech were cut off once again on all sides. Glyndwr's French allies controlled the Irish Sea and therefore no relief could be provided via the sea. Both Harlech and Criccieth surrendered to Glyndwr's forces.

Owain Glyndwr made his headquarters at Harlech, but had no need for Criccieth Castle, so it was burned.

The castle remained unmanned for years until 1858, when it was acquired by the Ormsby Gore family, who did some major repairs.

DENBIGH CASTLE, DENBIGHSHIRE

This castle is situated south of the town, on a site that is known as Denbigh Hill. Denbigh was the home of Dafydd ap Gruffydd, brother of Llywelyn, Prince of Wales. During Edward's army's push in North Wales in 1282, Denbigh, which was Dafydd's fortress, was captured by the King and given to Henry de Lucy, Earl of Lincoln. Work soon began in constructing a permanent stronghold and a wall to protect the town. Due to tragedy in de Lucy's family, work on the fortification stopped, leaving the town defenceless. In 1294, the Welsh attacked and burned the town. For the next few years, Denbigh had several owners, each one adding certain parts to the castle. One was Hugh le Despenser, perhaps the most unpopular Anglo-Norman in Wales.

During Edward I's reign, stone replaced the town's timber walls and the castle itself was built in the south-west corner. The outer walls are part of the town walls and therefore much thinner and less protected than the inner walls. There are four large round towers on the outer wall, with three octagonal towers and a large, three-towered gatehouse leading to the town. Also within its walls are a great hall and various other domestic buildings. To complete the castle defence there is a small barbican guarding the entrance, with a postern on the outer wall in the south-east corner.

In 1402, during Owain Glyndwr's uprising, Denbigh town was once again burned by his followers.

During the the Wars of the Roses, Denbigh often changed hands. In 1468, it was besieged by Henry Tudor, the half-brother of Jasper Tudor, Earl of Pembroke. After its destruction, the people decided to build the town in a safer place, outside the walls.

In 1563, during the reign of Elizabeth I, Robert Dudley, Earl of Leicester, became the owner of the castle. Dudley began in earnest to rebuild the castle, which had been seriously neglected.

The next conflict to hit Denbigh was the English Civil War, when the Royalists, under the command of Colonel Salisbury, garrisoned the castle. In 1645, Charles I visited the castle for three days while touring his troops in the area. Great effort was put into strengthening the castle and town walls to accommodate cannons. Denbigh eventually fell in 1646 to Major-General Mytton, the captor of Caernarfon and Conwy castles. In the wake of the war, the castle was left alone until the Restoration, when it was partially destroyed by gunpowder. Urgent repairs were done in the middle of the nineteenth century to make the castle safe.

HARLECH CASTLE, MERIONETH

This castle is regarded as one of the most majestic castles in Wales. It is perched high on a rock overlooking the sea. When it was built, the sea was at least half a mile closer to the rock on which it stands. The landward side of the castle is the most heavily protected, as the seaward side is naturally protected by a steep rock emerging from the water. Because of its strategic position, it has always been a prime target for both English and Welsh armies.

The crag of rock on which it stands was a site of an early hillfort.

The castle was built in 1283 by Edward I. As overland passage was dangerous, he had to bring most of the supplies and building material by sea. Initially, work was rather slow and difficult. By the time it was completed in 1290, 850 workmen had worked on the project.

The design of the castle was undertaken by Master James of St George, and for this great effort, he was made the first Constable of Harlech Castle (1290–93).

The inner walls of the eastern front are 12 feet thick. The others were much thinner, but had to be strengthened at a later date. The western tower and two turreted round towers guard the steep slope leading to the sea, overlooking a protected harbour built 200 feet below the castle walls at the bottom of the cliff. Several portcullises and thick wooden doors guarded the castle entrance. The narrow outer bailey was constructed with a low curtain, and follows the narrow ridge of the site.

In 1294, during Prince Madoc's uprising, a siege was lifted when reinforcement arrived by sea from Caernarfon and Conwy castles.

During Owain Glyndwr's 1400 uprising, the castle was again besieged, but as the French fleet commanded the sea around the Llyn Peninsula, reinforcements did not materialise. The siege lasted for a year and the occupants eventually surrendered. Glyndwr made Harlech his capital and held his first Welsh parliament there. In 1409, an English army of over 1,000 men recaptured the castle.

During the Wars of the Roses, the castle constable, Dafydd ap Ieuan, was a Lancastrian and therefore the castle was once again involved in a bitter struggle between the two houses. The Yorkist forces, led by Lord Herbert and his brother Sir Richard Herbert, besieged the castle. The occupants held out for a long time, but eventually surrendered because of famine. The courage of the occupants inspired the famous Welsh song 'Men of Harlech'.

With the accession of the Tudors to the throne, Wales experienced a period of peace and the castles fell into neglect.

With the outbreak of the English Civil War, Royalist sympathisers held most of the Welsh castles. Harlech was held by Sir Hugh Pennad and later by Colonel

William Owen, with only fifty men. They held out for most of the war. Harlech eventually surrendered to Parliamentarian forces in March 1647; it was the last of the Welsh castles to surrender.

KIDWELLY CASTLE, CARMARTHENSHIRE

This castle was built during the Normans' advance through South Wales. Henry I built a series of castles to split the Welsh leaders, but after his death the Welsh reunited. It was not until after the Battle of Maes Gwenllian in 1136 that the castle was strengthened. Initially it had a semicircular moat with a wall and earthworks, but most of the work was done in the late thirteenth and early fourteenth centuries.

The castle was frequently attacked and often captured by the Welsh, only to be recaptured by the Normans. According to Welsh chronicles, it was Lord Rhys who built the castle in 1190 (more likely it was during this period that some of the rebuilding took place). In 1201, the Normans were back in charge of the castle and, during one attempt to recapture it, Rhys's son Meredith was killed. His other son, Rhys Grug, burned the stronghold in 1215 and retook it in revenge for the death of his brother. The castle was held until 1222, when Llywelyn the Great forced Rhys to hand it back to the Normans in his bid for the acceptance of the nation.

When pacification failed during the reign of Henry III, the Welsh retook Kidwelly Castle, but lost it again some years later. Throughout the uprisings of 1257, the castle remained in Norman hands despite several attacks. In 1270, a major rebuilding programme took place, with a new wall and four towers built in the inner ward.

The next construction occurred under Henry, the Earl of Lancaster, who became the lord of Kidwelly Castle in 1291. A new chapel and new domestic quarter were built in the inner ward. An outer wall with large and small gatehouses and four round towers was constructed in a concentric pattern, similar to the design of other castles.

In 1399, upon the accession of Henry IV, Kidwelly Castle became the possession of the Crown and was given to Sir Rhys ap Tewdwr. Sir Rhys had to forfeit it in 1531, and the castle was passed on to the earls of Cawdor.

LLANSTEPHAN (LLANSTEFFAN) CASTLE, CARMARTHENSHIRE

This castle is situated on a hill overlooking the joint estuary of three rivers – the Taf, the Towy and the Gwendraeth. Its location, with a steep slope to the sea on the west side, made it a formidable fortification. There is evidence that the site was used during the Iron Age – there is a substantial bank and ditch to the west of the present castle. Further strong earthworks, dated to the late twelfth century, were built to form the round upper ward. A square three-storey gatehouse was added in the mid-thirteenth century, with a stone wall to protect the outer ward. Two round towers, a large bastion on the east corner, and a double-towered gatehouse were also built. In the fifteenth century, the gatehouse entrance was bricked up and a smaller entrance built nearby.

The Normans reached Carmarthen in around 1093, but did not achieve complete control until 1106. A series of fortifications were built near the sea or river estuaries, where they could be easily supplied.

Llansteffan Castle was attacked and captured by Maredudd, Rhys and Cadell in 1146, after their attack on the castle at Carmarthen.

The castle was handed down to Geoffrey Marmion, and then to William de Camville, who married Marmion's daughter.

Lord Rhys of South Wales captured the castle from de Camville for a short period in 1189, when he broke away from the English after the accession of Richard I. With the threat of another uprising, the castle defences were strengthened. However, after the Battle of Coed Llathen, the English army – made up mostly of Llansteffan Castle's garrison – was defeated, which left the castle defenceless. It was easily captured.

The next phase of the castle construction took place during Edward's invasion of Wales in the late thirteenth century, but the castle was not involved in the conflict. For the next few years, guardianship of the castle changed fairly often. The castle was captured by Owain Glyndwr's forces, but in 1408 it was recaptured by Sir John de Penres. For the next few centuries the ownership of the castle was rather complicated, resulting in great neglect.

MANORBIER CASTLE, PEMBROKESHIRE

This castle is situated off the A4139 and the B4585, in a very sheltered location with access to the sea.

The first castle to be built on the present site was at the beginning of the twelfth century, when the area was populated by the English during Henry I's reign. The first castle was a rectangular design with its customary great hall, small, round towers and a small, simple gatehouse. A thick wall with niches surrounded an inner ward. Its owner, John de Barri, made most of the modifications to the castle in the thirteenth century. It was built more along the lines of a baronial residence than as a stronghold, with emphasis on comfort and lavish interiors.

16. Manorbier Castle.

Manorbier Castle was the birthplace of Gerald de Barri, more commonly known as Giraldus Cambrensis (Gerald of Wales) – a renowned scholar, historian, traveller and writer who documented life in Wales at the time.

Manorbier Castle was rather fortunate not to be involved in serious military actions and does not bear the scars of battle.

The castle ownership remained with the Barri family until 1357. After that, its ownership changed several times until it was taken over by the Crown. The castle was sold to the Bowen family in the reign of Elizabeth I. During the English Civil War, the family stance was neutral, but nevertheless they took precautions – an earthen embankment and ditches reinforced with stones were constructed and the arrow slits in the towers and gatehouse were enlarged for the use of muskets and hand-held cannons.

MONMOUTH CASTLE, MONMOUTHSHIRE

William FitzOsbern, Earl of Hereford, built the town's first defence in around 1068. It was a typical Norman fortification with a simple motte and bailey, a wooden tower in an oval, ditched enclosure protected by a timber wall, and a wooden gatehouse. Soon a small town grew here, under the protection of the Norman garrison.

Between 1120 and 1150, the great tower, enclosed by a stone wall, was built to house the headquarters of the Marcher Lordship of Monmouth. In the first half of the twelfth century, John of Monmouth built a large, round tower.

The castle was captured by Richard Marshall, Earl of Pembroke, in 1233, as the result of a battle outside the town. During the reign of Edward I, the castle was captured by Simon de Montfort and his barons, but it was recaptured after de Montfort's army was defeated at Kenilworth. In 1267, the castle was handed to Edmund, the Earl of Lancaster, who built the great hall on the south side of the great tower. A royal birth took place here in 1387, when the future Henry V was born in the great tower.

During Owain Glyndwr's uprising, an English army was defeated at Craig y Dorth, near Monmouth, with the survivors pursued to the gates of the castle.

By 1550, the King's surveyors found the castle in a neglected state and regarded it as indefensible; only the great hall seemed to be habitable.

In the English Civil War, Monmouth Castle was garrisoned by Royalist troops, but fell to Parliamentarian forces under Colonel Massey in 1644. Within two months Massey was called away, and due to the loss of his leadership the castle fell to the King's men under Lord Charles Somerset. However, in October 1645, the garrison surrendered to an overwhelming force of Parliamentarian troops.

Parliament ordered the demolition of the castle and, together with the help of local people, the garrison pulled down the great tower. As was usual, large quantities of masonry were used in the construction of various buildings in the town.

PEMBROKE CASTLE, PEMBROKESHIRE

This castle is situated on a ridge, three of its sides surrounded by the River Cleddau. This position made a formidable site, since it had natural defences on four sides. The first stronghold built on the site was in 1093 by Roger of Montgomery. It consisted of a wooden tower and buildings protected by a strong timber and turf wall; even then it was able to withstand two sieges. William Marshall, Earl of Pembroke, began work on the stone castle and, after his death in 1219, it was continued over a thirty-year period by the various Earls of Pembroke. The resulting structure was a powerful fortress.

The castle has an irregular design, as the outer curtain, with five large round towers and a gatehouse, follows the shape of the rock it stands on. There was a gatehouse wall between the inner and outer baileys. A double wall was built on the south side of the outer curtain, where the defences were most vulnerable. Near the end of the twelfth century, a large, round keep was built inside the inner bailey, while the outer bailey consisted of towers, a gatehouse and two projected round towers on the east curtain, which was built in the mid-thirteenth century. The 80-foot, four-storey round keep had an imposing view over the rest of the castle and town. Also in the inner bailey were two large adjoining halls.

Between 1234 and 1241 William Marshall's son, Gilbert, enlarged and strengthened the castle. After years of belonging to the Marshall family, the castle came under the control of the Valence family, who held the castle for the next seventy years. It was during this period that the outer wall, complete with towers, was built and the town fortified with towers, three main gates and a postern.

With the death of Amer de Valence, the castle ownership reverted to Richard II.

In 1400, Owain Glyndwr was persuaded not to attack the town when offered a sum of money by the Constable of Pembroke.

In 1454, Henry VI passed on the castle to a new earl, his half-brother Jasper Tewdwr, who was the first earl to make his home at the castle. His sister-in-law Margaret was sent to Pembroke Castle, where she gave birth to a son, Henry Tudor.

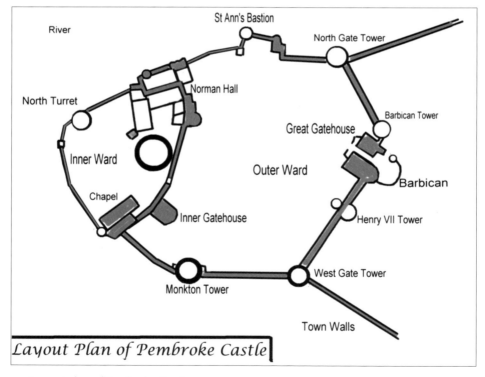

17. Layout plan of Pembroke Castle.

In 1485, Henry Tudor landed at Milford Haven with an army of over 2,000 and during his march north to claim his inheritance, his army doubled in size. At Bosworth on 22 August 1485, Henry's army defeated Richard's far larger force and the King was slain. Henry Tudor became Henry VII.

The period of peace that followed lasted until the English Civil War. When war broke out, Pembroke Castle was one of the few castles in Wales that did not support the King. The Mayor, a staunch Parliamentarian, garrisoned the castle for the cause.

During the Second English Civil War of 1648–49, the Mayor's allegiances changed and castle and town became a Royalist stronghold. In 1648, Cromwell's forces attacked the castle and after a six-week siege, the defenders surrendered. As a result of the Mayor's decision, a length of the castle wall was demolished.

Over the next few centuries, the castle fell into neglect, its functionality as a defensive stronghold giving way to new forts that were being built.

However, today the castle has been repaired and renovated. It is one of the great pre-Edwardian castles of Wales.

RAGLAN CASTLE, MONMOUTHSHIRE

According to some sources, this castle dates back to the mid-twelfth century. Other texts refer to a castle being built by Sir John Morley, who was Lord of Raglan Castle in around 1377. However, there is quite substantial evidence that the foundation of the present castle was put down in 1430, on the former site of a motte and bailey. No traditional castles were built after the Wars of the Roses; Raglan was the last of the great castles of Wales to be built. Its actual building is attributed to Sir William ap Thomas, who fought for Henry V at the Battle of Agincourt in 1415. The construction continued under the supervision of William Herbert, Earl of Pembroke and a supporter of the House of York.

The castle covers an area of four acres. It has an exceptional six-sided keep surrounded by a stone wall. Initially, there was a small gatehouse leading into the outer ward, but it was bricked up and replaced by a large, twin-towered gatehouse. Another three large and two smaller multi-angular towers, typical of the Tudor architecture of the time, were built.

During the Wars of the Roses, William Herbert was captured by the Lancastrians and executed.

Over the next decades, no further work was done at the castle and it fell into neglect.

The castle featured strongly in Charles I's campaign in South Wales. After the Royalist defeat at Naseby, the King stayed at the castle. After the surrender of

18. Raglan Castle.

Monmouth Castle, Parliamentarian forces headed for Raglan and after a long siege in 1646 by Sir Thomas Fairfax and 3,500 troops, the garrison surrendered, ending the English Civil War in South Wales. The castle was dismantled, with is stones and timber taken to Monmouth and Bristol to repair the damage done by the war. During the English Civil War, various alterations were made at the castle to render it suitable for modern warfare – arrow slits in the bastions were enlarged for the use of muskets and hand-held cannons, and the battlements' walkways were enlarged with timber to suit cannons.

RHUDDLAN CASTLE, FLINTSHIRE

There has been a fortification at Rhuddlan since the eighth century, at a place known as Twthill; it was captured by English forces in AD 796. The stronghold became the seat of Gruffydd ap Llywelyn until the Saxon leader Harold Godwinsson destroyed it in 1063.

The first Norman fortification dates back to around 1073, when a typical Norman motte-and-bailey castle with timber walls and buildings occupied the site. Robert of Rhuddlan built the first true castle south of the present site.

The site chosen was of great strategic importance as it controlled a vast area and had sea access.

In 1277, Edward I's army swept across large areas of Wales. In order to control his territory, he built castles. Work began on the present castle on 14 September 1277, with most of it completed by 1282. Design and supervision of the construction was done by Master James of St George, the King's master castle builder. By the time of the Welsh uprising in 1282, the outer defences had been completed.

It was a concentrically planned castle with a diamond-shaped inner ward and, unusually, two-towered gatehouses on two of the corners. There were also two round towers on the other two corners. The inner ward had six well-protected towers, while the wide outer ward sloped steeply to the river. The castle had a moat on three sides, which was flooded by the tide. The river provided protection on the remaining side.

The outer curtain had a number of turrets and four gates, with one large tower guarding the river dock and the river itself.

The town was defended by a timber and earthwork built between 1280 and 1282.

Rhuddlan Castle was not involved in the various Welsh uprisings, but Owain Glyndwr's forces destroyed the town in 1400.

During the English Civil War, the castle was garrisoned for the Royalists; however, in 1646 it surrendered to Parliamentarian forces and was wrecked in 1648.

WHITE CASTLE, LLANTILLO CROSSENNY, MONMOUTHSHIRE

Perhaps one of the best-preserved castles of the Marches, White Castle was part of a ring of strongholds built by the Normans between 1138 and 1155 for the defence of Gwent. Originally known as Llantilio Castle, it was classed as a ring type, initially with a low inner ward and a small half-moon shaped bailey defended by strong earthworks. The inner ward, which had a square keep, was protected by a timber wall and a moat.

In the middle of the thirteenth century, the castle was more or less rebuilt with a substantial stone wall protected by six round towers at set intervals around the ward. A gatehouse was placed between two of the towers. A moat was built around the inner ward with a new large bailey protected by a deep ditch. For defence, a stone wall, a fortified gate, three round towers and a rectangular tower protected the outer bailey.

In 1201, the castle was granted to Hubert de Burgh by King John, and in 1205 it transferred to William de Braose. For the next few years the castle changed hands several times; by 1234, it was no longer a possession of the Crown. Most of the reconstruction was done in 1244. It was eventually given to Prince Edward, who became Edward I and spent a fortune improving the castle's defences. When the Welsh threat had been removed, the castle had no further military importance and was left to ruin.

SOME LESSER-KNOWN CASTLES

This list includes castles that are in either ruins or are referred to in historical documents. As with the previous chapter, the list does not include walled strongholds or fortified manors. Also not included are Iron Age or Roman fortifications. There are hundreds of places in Wales with either 'castle' or the Welsh word 'castell' in their names but no evidence of castle-type structure. In most cases, the origins of the name are very vague.

ABER CASTLE, GWYNEDD

This small castle, situated about five miles east of Bangor, dates back to 1090 and only consists of a mound of earth.

ABEREDW CASTLE, POWYS

This castle became one of the centres of resistance to Edward's occupation of Wales and became a favourite retreat with Llewelyn, Prince of Wales, when he visited the north.

The first fortification built on the site dates back to around 1093, when it was funded by the Baskerville family during the Norman push across Mid- and South Wales. The original castle was a simple motte-and-bailey type with a deep ditch surrounding the site. The defences were strengthened with a curtain stone wall and towers. By the thirteenth century, the castle was controlled by the Welsh, who put their own stamp on the structure. After a series of battles, it was captured by the English, who fortified the castle defences. As other castles were built in the area, its importance declined and it fell into neglect and, eventually, ruins.

ABERGAVENNY CASTLE, MONMOUTHSHIRE

The actual date of this castle, especially the motte and bailey, goes back to around 1067–68, soon after the Norman invasion of Britain. It was founded by Hameline de Balun. The present castle was built in around 1100, but changed ownership in 1172, when Syllt ap Dyferwald took possession. Soon afterwards it was restored to its original owner. After a period of treachery and the murder of Welsh chieftains, the Welsh attacked and burned the castle.

During the reign of King John and the baronial revolt in 1215, the castle was restored and occupied by the King's supporters, but was then captured by Llywelyn ap Iorwerth. The castle was in the thick of battle again in 1403, when Owain Glyndwr's forces burned the town.

After years of peace, the ruins were used again during the English Civil War.

ABERLLEINOG CASTLE, LLANGOED, ANGLESEY

A low motte-and-bailey type castle was built at Llangoed in about 1088 by the Earl of Chester.

ANGLE CASTLE, PEMBROKESHIRE

Situated in the village of Angle, this stronghold was built in the fourteenth century as secure family accommodation. It's a single fortified round tower with the usual arrow slits and roof battlements.

BARRY CASTLE, BARRY, GLAMORGAN

This was a small fortified manorial residence built in the fourteenth century and is situated on the west edge of town.

BEAUPRE CASTLE, ST HILARY, GLAMORGANSHIRE

The Basset family, who were descendants of the first Norman settlers, built Beaupre Castle in the thirteenth century and held on to the property until 1709. The family managed to keep out of Owain Glyndwr's uprisings, and therefore the castle escaped any involvement whatsoever.

When the Basset family left the castle in the sixteenth century, it fell into neglect and disrepair. In 1586, an Elizabethan manor was built on the site using material from the castle. In 1643, Sir Richard Basset, a supporter of the King, was made High Sheriff. In 1645, he was appointed the governor of Cardiff Castle. He was captured by Parliamentarian forces in Hereford and, after paying a fine, he was unable to keep Beaupre Manor. The last member of the Basset family to live in the manor was the grandson of Sir Richard.

BENTON CASTLE, LLANGWM, PEMBROKESHIRE

This was a small enclosure castle with a round keep and one round tower built in the late thirteenth century.

BLEFFDA CASTLE, POWYS

This castle is located some ten miles from Llandridnod Wells on the A488 road. The castle dates back to late twelfth century and consisted of a small bailey and motte. It was more of an outpost stronghold than a castle, and was attacked and captured in 1262.

BOUGHROOD CASTLE, POWYS

Another small castle, consisting of one round tower and a low bailey, was built in Powys in 1205.

19. Pales Tower in Angle.

BOVEHILL CASTLE, CHERITON, GLAMORGAN

This castle is situated on Nottle Tor, a prominent limestone spar overlooking marshland. It was built by the Normans during their occupation of the Gower area.

BRONLLYS CASTLE, BRECONSHIRE

This was a knight's stronghold, built in the thirteenth century. It consisted of a round keep and two baileys, one of stone and the other timber. The stronghold was first documented in 1175 and was involved in local uprisings in 1233 and 1322.

BUILTH CASTLE, BUILTH WELLS, BRECONSHIRE

This castle, one of the eight built by Edward I to control his realm, is situated at the east end of the town.

It is believed that there was a stronghold on the site as far back as 1168. Edward's castle was built in 1219 and consisted of a round keep on a substantial motte; the initial large bailey was divided into two at a later date. A missionary wall protected the motte tower and the main bailey was comprised of stone and timber. The castle's main protection was its earth works, a wet moat and a strong counterscarp bank, which surrounded the site.

Within four years of its construction, the castle was attacked and damaged. In 1260, while under the control of Sir Roger Mortimer, the castle was captured and destroyed by Welsh forces. After it had been recaptured, the castle defences were strengthened in 1277.

CAERLEON CASTLE, MONMOUTHSHIRE

This castle is situated three miles north-east of Newport, on the site of a settlement and fortifications established by the Celts and Romans. In 1085, the Normans constructed a steep motte with a tower and a two-towered barbican at the bottom, plus a bailey. Another two towers were added in the thirteenth century. The castle was attacked and captured and recaptured in 1217 and attacked again in 1231. After that, the castle's importance declined.

CAERWRLE CASTLE, FLINTSHIRE

This small castle is situated six miles south-east of Mold. It was built in the thirteenth century with three half round towers and a small defensive turret set in part of a large earthwork enclosure of an earlier hillfort.

CALDICOT CASTLE, MONMOUTHSHIRE

This was a Norman stronghold built on the site of a Saxon castle at the beginning of the twelfth century. It had the usual Norman round keep on a large motte, and an outer wall with four round towers. One was used as a gatehouse. A lavish hall and two gates were added in the fourteenth century.

CANDLESTON CASTLE, MERTHYRMAWR, GLAMORGAN

This castle is situated three miles from Bridgend and was built in the fourteenth century. It had a square tower and a polygonal courtyard. A fortified building was added a century later for accommodation.

CARDIGAN CASTLE, CEREDIGION

The present ruin was built on the site of a castle by Rhys ap Gruffydd, whose main claim to fame was organising a festival of Welsh bards at Christmas 1176, a forerunner of the Welsh Eisteddfod.

The castle was in a prominent position, for it controlled access to the River Teifi and the Teifi Valley, which led into the hinterland. Most of the infrastructure left today is from the major rebuilding that took place afterwards. The circular keep and the series of round towers were built on a rocky crag overlooking the river. The castle was further fortified in around 1249 and again during the reign of Edward I, who is believed to have stayed at the castle.

During the English Civil War, and like most of the Welsh castles, Cardigan supported the Royalist cause but surrendered after a short siege. The Parliamentarians wrecked the castle, making sure it could not be used again.

CARDIGAN OLD CASTLE, CEREDIGION

There were two castles in Cardigan; the old one located a mile south-west from the town, and the other in the town itself.

Roger of Montgomery built Cardigan Old Castle in 1093, just after the Norman advance into West Wales. An early stronghold on the site is believed to have been the home of Cadwgan, Prince of Powys, and it was utilised in the defence against the Normans. The stronghold was burned and destroyed in 1165, but was rebuilt with locally mined stones in 1171. Between 1198 and 1231, the castle was captured and recaptured five times. Like a number of smaller castles in Wales, its importance diminished and the structure was left to ruin.

CASTELL CARNOCHAN, LLANUWCHLLYN, GWYNEDD

This Welsh-built castle with a D-shaped keep was built in the mid-thirteenth century.

CASTELL COCH, TONGWYNLAIS, GLAMORGAN

This small castle originally had a triangular layout on a low motte, with a round tower at each corner. The curtain wall was slightly curved and had numerous arrow slits. Work began on the castle in 1260 and was not completed until the middle of the fourteenth century. The castle's claim to fame is the red stone used to build it.

CASTELL COCH, YSTRADFELLTE, BRECONSHIRE

This castle was built in around 1225 on a sharp ridge with a panoramic view of the area. It was a small, walled fortification with a round tower and a hall.

CASTELL CWM ARAN, LLANDEWI YSTRADENNY, POWYS

This small Norman castle was rebuilt after an attack in 1144. Over the following years it was attacked and damaged several times, requiring extensive repairs.

CASTELL DDINAS, GENFORDD, POWYS

Located some eight miles east of Brecon, this castle was built in the twelfth century on the site of a hillfort. Inside the castle's inner ward there were at least three small, rectangular towers. The Welsh forces took the castle in 1233.

CASTELL DINAS BRAN, LLANGOLLEN, DENBIGHSHIRE

It is believed that Gruffydd ap Madoc built this castle in 1236. It consisted of a large, square keep in a rectangular courtyard, with a twin-towered gatehouse and a large D-shaped tower. The walls are built of small slate-type stones set in mortar. The castle has been included in a number of Welsh stories and exploits. It was captured from the Welsh in 1277, recaptured soon afterwards, and captured again by the English in 1282. Under the stewardship of Thomas Fitzalan, the Earl of Arundel, it was besieged by Owain Glyndwr. During the reign of Henry VIII, the castle was left to fall into ruin.

CASTELL DINAS EMRYS, BEDDGELERT, GWYNEDD

This Welsh-built castle consisting of a square tower dates back to the beginning of the thirteenth century.

CASTELL GWALLTER, LLANDRE, CEREDIGION

This castle is located four miles from Aberystwyth, on the B4353. It was a small castle set on a hill with a low motte and a ditch cut into the rock. According to old documents it was attacked and destroyed in 1136, but it was apparently repaired, as it is mentioned again in 1151.

CASTELL MACHEN, MACHEN UPPER, MONMOUTHSHIRE

This castle is located on a rocky ridge near to Caerphilly. It was built in the early thirteenth century by the Welsh. It was typically Welsh, with a round tower and a walled bailey in front.

CASTELL MEURIG (LLANGADOG CASTLE), LLANGADOG, CARMARTHENSHIRE

This Welsh castle was mostly involved in feuds between various Welsh leaders. Over the years between 1209 and 1277, it changed hands several times, culminating in its complete destruction when Edward I's army captured the town in 1277.

CASTELL MOR CRAIG, THORN HILL, GLAMORGAN

This castle that was never completed, nor inhabited. Gruffydd ap Rhys began work on the castle in the mid-thirteenth century. Evidence suggests the castle was to have four round towers of different sizes and a square keep.

CASTELL Y BERE, LLANFIHANGEL-Y-PENNANT

This castle is situated halfway between Dolgellau and Tywyn and in its day it was the largest and most important castle in Wales. Construction was begun by Llywelyn the Great in 1221. After the Treaty of Rhuddlan in 1277, Dafydd, the brother of Llywelyn, made his base at the castle. In the war of 1282, Llywelyn was killed and Castell y Bere became the last point of resistance in the area. Dafydd was captured and the castle surrendered to the English, who destroyed it in 1294.

CRICKHOWELL CASTLE, CRICKHOWELL, BRECONSHIRE

Initially this was a simple motte-and-bailey castle with timber walls and buildings. In the thirteenth century, it was completely rebuilt with a keep on the motte, a gatehouse and a stone wall with two towers circling the outer ward. Further construction took place in the fourteenth century. It was captured by the Welsh in 1322, but was soon recaptured.

DEGANWY CASTLE, CONWY

The site of this castle overlooks the Conwy Estuary and the present Conwy Castle. The castle was built on two large volcanic rocks.

The builders made good use of the outcrop, as it provided natural defence for the castle. The Welsh ruler Maelgwyn, King of Gwynedd, built the first fortification on the site in the early sixth century. Built mostly of timber, the stronghold was severely damaged by lightning in the early ninth century. The site was taken over in 1088 by the Norman baron Hugh de Lupus, the Earl of Chester, who built a small castle on the site. It was attacked and destroyed by Llywelyn the Great's forces in 1241.

Because of its strategic site, Henry III had the castle rebuilt in 1245 with more prominent defence, including a D-shaped tower on the smaller hillock and a large, double-towered gatehouse. Llywelyn, the last Prince of Wales, was responsible for a long siege in 1263. Eventually the English surrendered and the castle was demolished. In 1283, most of the stones were used in the construction of Conwy Castle.

DINEFWR CASTLE, LLANDEILO, CARMARTHEN

This castle is situated a mile from the town of Llandeilo. The thirteenth-century castle was built on the site of a fort built by Rhodri the Great in around AD 876, at a time when the principality was divided into three great kingdoms – Gwynedd, Powys and Deheubarth. The stronghold became an important site for Rhys ap Tewdwr, who held it against the first Norman invasion of South Wales. The original castle was demolished and rebuilt around 1230 with a

20. Dinefwr Castle.

large, round keep, a small tower, and a rectangular hall built alongside the chamber block and protruding out beyond the curtain wall. A great hall, along with other minor buildings, was built in the fourteenth century. In 1403 Owain Glyndwr besieged the castle, but he was not able to capture it. The castle was abandoned in the mid-fifteenth century.

DOLBADARN CASTLE, LLANBERIS, GWYNEDD

Dolbadarn, one of the castles of the Welsh princes, is situated some 80 feet above Llyn Padarn in the Llanberis Pass. The castle was built in a strategic position on a rocky hillock with a clear view of the area. The Welsh prince Llywelyn ap Iorwerth built it in the thirteenth century (before 1230), although the site had been of military importance since as far back as the sixth century.

A 50-foot-high, 40-foot-diameter round tower or keep was built by Llywelyn, enclosed in a wall that followed the rocky hilltop and took advantage of the steep drop on the sides. Two rectangular towers were built as part of the curtain wall; there was also a large hall. The castle construction was mostly of slate stone and rubble.

According to records, it was active until 1300. In 1250, it was used to imprison Owain ap Gruffydd, the younger brother of Hywel the Great. He remained imprisoned there for at least twenty years.

During Edward I's invasion of Wales, Dolbadarn was held by Dafydd ap Gruffydd until 1282. However, it was eventually captured by the Earl of Pembroke and a large English army.

In 1284, Dolbadarn was abandoned after the building of castles at Caernarfon and Conwy. The ruins were used briefly by Owain Glyndwr's forces in 1400.

DOLFORWYN CASTLE, ABERMULE, MONTGOMERYSHIRE

This castle was built by Llywelyn, the last Prince of Wales, deep in the English heartland. The castle, of a rectangular construction, was situated on a ridge, taking full advantage of the local topography. It consisted of a large round tower surrounded by a wall. After Edward's conquest of Wales in 1282, the castle was granted to Sir Roger Mortimer.

21. Dolwyddelan Castle.

DOLWYDDELAN CASTLE, GWYNEDD

This castle is situated strategically on a high escarpment overlooking the Lledr Valley, some five miles south-west of Betws y Coed. Llywelyn's father Iorwerth built the castle in 1170. It consisted of a tower, stone buildings, a stone wall, and a strong ditch defence, taking full advantage of the rocky site. Two larger rectangular towers linked by an irregular curtain wall were built at a later date.

Dolwyddelan Castle is traditionally the birthplace of the Welsh hero Llywelyn the Great. He joined the barons in their revolt against King John in 1215 and was able to gain recognition of Welsh rights in the Magna Carta. From his base at Dolwyddelan, he had absolute control over the other Welsh princes.

DRYSLWYN CASTLE, CARMARTHENSHIRE

This thirteenth-century castle is built on a natural hillock overlooking the Towy Valley, some five miles west of Llandeilo. The site occupied an earlier castle built by Rhys ap Gruffydd, who withstood an Anglo-Norman army in the twelfth century. The present ruins are of a castle built around 1246, consisting of a round tower or a keep adjoining a polygonal wall and enclosed within a stone curtain wall. It had a simple, well-protected gateway entrance on the north-eastern side. Inside the courtyard, there were a series of stone buildings, including a large hall and a chapel. Rhys ap Maredudd, who resisted the growing influence and power of Llywelyn ap Gruffydd (the Prince of Wales), allied himself with Edward

I's campaign against Llywelyn. Instead of being rewarded, Rhys lost all of his territories with the exception of Dryslwyn Castle. In 1287, Rhys raised a large army and captured Dinefwr, Carreg Cennen and Llandovery castles, but due to the overwhelming English forces, he was defeated. He escaped to Ireland and returned in 1290, but was defeated again and finally executed in York.

EWLOE CASTLE, FLINTSHIRE

This castle is located some two miles from Hawarden and near to the large fortresses of Flint and Rhuddlan. Originally it was built by the English near Offa's Dyke, marking the boundary between the two countries. With the capture of Mold in 1146 by Owain Gwynedd, Ewloe became Welsh as well.

The castle was built to the standard Welsh design of the time. A motte and bailey with a D-shaped keep was added in around 1200.

Ewloe remained in various Welsh hands for a considerable period. Based at the castle, Llywelyn ap Gruffydd was able to regain control of the border areas.

When Llywelyn became Prince of Wales, he strengthened its walls and tower. A second ward was built down a slope, with a round tower at the end. When Edward I invaded North Wales, Llywelyn lost a number of his strongholds and lands and Ewloe was besieged. By 1277, Llywelyn had arranged a peace treaty with Edward, who began building a large castle at Flint, making Ewloe unimportant.

FLINT CASTLE, FLINTSHIRE

After the signing of a one-sided treaty at Rhuddlan Castle between Llywelyn and Edward I, the King soon established his authority over the Welsh by building a series of strongholds in the area. The first was at Flint in 1277. Over 950 men were employed on the construction of ditches and earthwork at a cost equivalent to £100,000 in just one month. The castle was a typical Norman design with a square inner bailey with four corner towers and one large tower, or donjon (a round keep), defended on one side by a moat and drawbridge. The donjon, being the main building of the castle, housed a chapel, banquet room, store and accommodation for the nobles.

The castle was completed in 1280, but within two years it was attacked by the Welsh, who captured the outer defences. The Welsh were defeated and the English secured the castle once more. Eventually, Flint Castle would be superseded in importance by other castles in North Wales.

22. Flint Castle.

FONMON CASTLE, PENMARK, GLAMORGAN

This castle four miles west of Barry was initially built in the thirteenth century, but was rebuilt in the fourteenth. The castle had two round towers and a square tower surrounded by a stone wall.

GROSMONT, MONMOUTHSHIRE

This castle is nine miles north-east of the town of Abergavenny. It was one of three castles built to defend the Monmow Valley and protect the English plains from the Welsh. The other two castles were Skenfirth Castle and White Castle.

The castle was built on the site of an earlier Norman stronghold dating back to about 1070. The next phase of the rebuilding, initiated by Hubert de Burgh, took place around 1136–1201. Further work took place between 1274 and 1294 involving an inner ward, a gatehouse and two round towers on the wall, with a deep ditch surrounding the castle. The great hall was built in the early thirteenth century during a rebuilding programme; it also acted as the castle keep.

Owain Glyndwr's army captured Grosmont Castle, but under Rhys Gethin it was lost in 1410 to Henry of Monmouth, who became Henry V.

HAVERFORDWEST CASTLE, PEMBROKESHIRE

This castle was built on a rocky crag overlooking the River Cleddau, which at the time was the highest point on the river that was navigable. It was built in the thirteenth century by a Norman baron, William de Valence, but according to some sources it was Gilbert de Clare who first built a castle on the site in the twelfth century. The first castle was burned and destroyed by Llywelyn the Great in 1220. In 1405, it was the town that was burned by Owain Glyndwr, although the castle escaped destruction.

During the English Civil War the Royalist garrison at the castle fled when it heard that the garrison at Milford Haven had surrendered to Parliamentarians. Cromwell ordered Haverfordwest town's people to destroy the castle, but owing to a lack of money, men and gunpowder, only partial demolition took place.

HAY CASTLE, HAY-ON-WYE, BRECONSHIRE

The castle is believed to have been built around 1100 by a knight named Revell – one of Henry I's men. The castle consisted of a motte and bailey. However, it was strengthened in the thirteenth century with an extended wall and a gateway. The residential section was built during the reign of Elizabeth I.

HEN BLAS CASTLE, FLINTSHIRE

The site of this castle is situated on an intersection of two valleys about a mile from the town of Flint. It had an inner ward and a large outer courtyard built on a substantial earthwork. It dates back to the early thirteenth century and was constructed mostly of timber, with a few stone structures.

HOLT CASTLE, HOLT, DENBIGHSHIRE

The castle was built in the thirteenth century in a strategic position on the English/Welsh border. There is evidence that the site was used in the Bronze Age and during the Roman occupation. The castle was built by the Earl of Surrey, John de Warenne, towards the end of the century. It was of a pentagonal design, with round towers built on the outside of the wall. The castle changed sides often during the First English Civil War of 1642–46.

KENFIG CASTLE, GLAMORGAN

This castle, built in the twelfth century by Robert, Earl of Gloucester, is situated five miles south-west of Port Talbot. The Earl also established a settlement nearby. According to excavations, the castle had a substantial square keep on a fortified motte. Towards the end of the thirteenth century, a narrow wall was built around the tower; a large bailey with a protected gatehouse was also built, enclosing the town within its walls. The castle was burned during an attack in 1295 and was captured by local rebels in 1321. In the end, the castle and the settlement were overwhelmed by the sand dunes creeping inland.

LAUGHARNE CASTLE, CARMARTHENSHIRE

This castle is situated on the mouth of the River Taf and its origins go back to a small stronghold established on the site in 1116. Throughout its history, Laugharne Castle was constantly captured and retaken. The castle consisted of a round tower keep and a smaller defensive tower, which were built toward the end of the thirteenth century. A gatehouse was added at a later date.

The first recorded holder of the castle was Sir Guy de Brian in the early fourteenth century. During the reign of Henry VIII, the then-owner, Sir John Perrot, incorporated most of the old castle into a fortified mansion.

LLANDOVERY CASTLE, CARMARTHENSHIRE

Richard Fitz Pons built this castle in the twelfth century. It consisted of a fortified stone keep and stone and timber walls. In 1116, the stronghold was captured by the Welsh, who held it until the English recaptured it in 1272. Over the next fifteen years, the castle changed hands four times. It was finally attacked and damaged by Owain Glyndwr's forces in 1403.

LLANFAIR DISCOED CASTLE, MONMOUTHSHIRE

This castle was built in the late twelfth or early thirteenth century, about ten miles north-east of what is now Newport. The castle consisted of a courtyard and various buildings, surrounded by a wall, at least two towers and a gatehouse.

LLANGIBBY CASTLE (CASTELL TREGRUG), LLANGYBI, MONMOUTHSHIRE

This castle was built on a large summit site in the early fourteenth century. The castle had only one large ward, with an elongated fortified keep in the middle. There was a gatehouse with numerous arrow slits and four round towers. At the opposite end to the gatehouse were a smaller gatehouse and a turret.

LLANQUIAN CASTLE, COWBRIDGE, GLAMORGAN

This was a small motte-and-bailey castle.

LLANTRISANT CASTLE, GLAMORGAN

Richard de Clare built this castle after the Welsh leader Hywel ap Meredith was deposed in 1245. The Welsh attacked it in 1315 and 1316 and it was badly damaged.

The castle consisted of a small inner bailey with a large, round, fortified keep and a large outer bailey. It was built in a strategic position between two hills overlooking the Vale of Ely. Edward II was captured near the castle during his escape from Queen Isabella and held there.

The castle was used as a prison during the Tudor reign.

LLAWADEN CASTLE, PEMBROKESHIRE

This castle is rich in history. Its earliest part can be traced back to Queen Matilda's reign, when a ring motte was built to protect the estate of one of the Queen's chaplains, Bernard, who was elected bishop in 1115. At first, the castle was a wooden stockade with a few stone buildings. By the time the castle was captured in 1192, stone walls and towers had been built. Most of the castle was destroyed by 1194, but it was reclaimed by the bishop and totally rebuilt with semicircular towers and a 70-foot-wide, nearly 25-foot-deep moat. During the early fourteenth century, the castle went through a period of rebuilding and updating. The finished construction provided the bishop with lavish and comfortable accommodation. An extension of the gatehouse was carried out towards the end of the century. It remained the bishop's residence well into the 1500s. According to some sources, Bishop Barlow dismantled the castle in the mid-sixteenth century because he felt it was too lavish for a man of the cloth.

LOUGHOR CASTLE, GLAMORGAN

This castle is located four miles from Llanelli. It is situated on a natural mound of earth, near where the River Loughor can be crossed. The Norman castle was fairly small, with a stone curtain and a large square tower, or keep. The original Norman castle was destroyed in 1151; it was rebuilt and captured in 1215. It seems it was repaired, as it is mentioned in various documents in around 1391.

MAENCLOCHOG CASTLE

The middle of the village of Maenclochog is the possible site of a small early eleventh-century motte-and-bailey castle.

MATHRAFAL CASTLE, MEIFOD, POWYS

This castle is situated some six miles north-west of Welshpool. It had a low motte within a square earthwork with timber walls and buildings. The castle was built and destroyed in 1212.

MONTGOMERY CASTLE, POWYS

The original Montgomery Castle was built on the order of Roger de Montgomery, the Earl of Shrewsbury between 1071 and 1074. Initially it was a simple motte-and-bailey type with wooden structures. After several attacks and its eventual destruction by Llywelyn ap Iorwerth in 1215, a new castle was built by Henry III in 1223, located some distance away on a rocky hill near the town. The castle consisted of an inner ward with a fortified gatehouse and two D-shaped towers on the curtain wall of the ward. After a successful attack by Prince Llywelyn in 1228, the castle defences were improved with the addition of middle and outer wards. In 1229, the Crown gave the castle to Hubert de Burgh. It was attacked in 1233 and considerable damage was done to the Well Tower, which had to be rebuilt.

In 1267, a treaty was signed at the castle between Henry III and Llywelyn, granting the latter the title Prince of Wales.

With that constant threat of an uprising, the castle was fortified and refurbished by Roger Mortimer in 1400.

By the Tudor period, the castle had been handed down to the Herbert family, who supported the King during the English Civil War. Lord Herbert of Cherbury, who garrisoned the castle, surrendered to Parliamentarian forces in 1644. The castle was demolished in 1649, after the end of the Second English Civil War.

NARBERTH CASTLE, NARBERTH, PEMBROKESHIRE

This site, according to the *Mabinogion*, was the home of Pwyll, Prince of Dyfed.

The first Norman fortification was a wooden construction built in around 1116. The rectangular stone castle was built by Sir Andrew Parrot in the thirteenth century and consisted of a single ward with a keep and four round towers situated on the wall. Other buildings, including a gatehouse and a hall, were added later. In 1404, Thomas Carrewe defended the castle against Owain Glyndwr's followers with a small garrison, and for his devotion he was given a lordship. Another castle guardian was Sir Edmund Mortimer, who strengthened and fortified the castle during his time there.

NEVERN CASTLE (CASTELL NANHYFER), PEMBROKESHIRE

This Norman castle was built in 1191. It was a strong motte-and-bailey stronghold with stone and wooden buildings – a typical structure built during the Norman invasion of Wales.

A stone wall and a rocky ditch protected a square tower and a timber wall with wooden towers protected the outer ward. It was captured and recaptured in a short time. During an attack in 1195, the structure was badly burned and was abandoned.

NEWCASTLE EMLYN CASTLE, CARMARTHENSHIRE

The castle was located in the district of Emlyn, which was under the control of William Marshal, Earl of Pembroke. The original castle, built in the thirteenth century, consisted of a four-sided wall with an outer enclosure. In 1347–49, the English enlarged its defences with a double-towered gatehouse and a small polygonal tower. In 1403, Owain Glyndwr's forces took the castle, resulting in considerable damage to the infrastructure. By the time Henry VII gave the castle to Rhys ap Thomas, it had fallen into neglect.

In 1485, it was rebuilt and became one of his residences. During the English Civil War the castle was held by Royalists, but after a siege it was captured by Parliamentarians.

NEWPORT CASTLE, MONMOUTHSHIRE

This castle, built by the Normans in 1172, is situated in Newport on the River Usk. The original castle was only a temporary stronghold, and it was completely rebuilt during the fourteenth and fifteenth centuries. It was a square stone castle containing the bridge tower and a central tower containing the water gate and a chapel. The castle was captured and retaken several times, the last time by Owain Glyndwr in 1404.

NEWPORT CASTLE, PEMBROKESHIRE

This castle was built in the early thirteenth century by William de Turribus to replace nearby Nevern Castle. The castle had three round towers; it is believed that the largest was the keep. An impressive twin-towered gatehouse was added in the later part of the century. The various revolts in Wales did not seem to reach this part of Pembrokeshire, and therefore the castle was not attacked. Most of the castle stone was used to build a mansion in 1859.

OGMORE CASTLE, GLAMORGAN

This castle is situated two miles south-west of Bridgend, near the mouth of the River Ogmore. It was built in a strategically important position on the banks of the river, forming a defence of the western boundary of the county of Glamorgan. The castle guarded the trade routes across the Ogmore and the Ewenny.

The stronghold dates back to the early twelfth century, with some of the other structures pre-Norman, including the three-storey rectangular tower.

During the Norman occupation, further domestic buildings were added and surrounded by a walled courtyard. The castle was further protected by earthwork defences and a moat on three sides, with the River Ewenny providing a natural defence. William de Londres built the original basic fortification in 1116–17. The castle was shaped by William's son Maurice, who also took control of Kidwelly Castle.

Soon afterwards, the family fortunes were tied up in their new acquisition in Kidwelly. A courthouse was built in the fifteenth century and the castle was also used as a prison.

OXWICH CASTLE, GLAMORGAN

The castle is situated some eleven miles south-west of Swansea. The castle consisted of a curtain, a gatehouse and a round tower. This early castle belonged to a wealthy family of landowners and was handed down to members of the family. The owners incurred the displeasure of Edward III and lost their estate to the Crown, during which time it fell into neglect. In the sixteenth century, a large manor house was built on the site, mostly using masonry from the castle.

OYSTERMOUTH CASTLE, MUMBLES, GLAMORGAN

During their advance through Glamorgan, the Normans built the first castle at Oystermouth.

The Welsh destroyed the castle in 1116, and again in 1215. Reconstruction by William de Braoces took place in the thirteenth century with a strengthened two-towered gatehouse and a large three-storey rectangular tower, which contained a hall, a chapel and domestic rooms. The east and west walls were of exceptional height, deterring any attacker.

PAINSCASTLE, POWYS

This is a typical example of a strong motte-and-bailey castle, with at least one round tower, or keep, on the motte. Payn Fitzjohn built the castle in around 1137. At the end of the twelfth century, it was held by William de Braose and was besieged by Gwenwynwyn of Powys. Painscastle was captured in 1215 and during its rebuilding in 1231 it was strengthened with several D-shaped towers. After another attack in 1265, it was badly damaged.

PENHOW CASTLE, MONMOUTHSHIRE

This was a small fortification with a ward and oblong tower built in thirteenth century. In the fifteenth century, a round tower was added and the wall strengthened.

PICTON CASTLE, HAVERFORDWEST, PEMBROKESHIRE

William de Picton, a Norman knight, built the first castle on the site during the reign of William II. It was a substantial fortress with four attached round towers on each corner and a small double-towered gatehouse. It did not have an internal courtyard. The castle dates from the end of the thirteenth century.

During the English Civil War, Sir Richard Phillipps, a supporter of the King, garrisoned his soldiers at the castle, but after a long siege the defenders surrendered.

ROCH CASTLE, PEMBROKESHIRE

This castle at Roch was founded in the latter part of the thirteenth century by Adam de Rupe, although a fortress existed on the site in around 1200. The castle consisted of a D-shaped tower built on a rocky outcrop. From 1420 onwards,

23. Roch Castle.

the castle changed ownership several times until it became the possession of the Walter family. During the English Civil War, the castle was a Royalist stronghold. It was captured by Parliamentarians, recaptured by the King's supporters, and fell again to Cromwell's forces. After the English Civil War, the castle was neglected and fell into ruins. In 1900, Viscount St David acquired the property and made major restorations.

RUTHIN CASTLE, DENBIGHSHIRE

This impressive baronial castle was built between 1277 and 1282 by order of Edward I. It consisted of a large inner ward and a smaller outer ward with five round towers and a double-towered gatehouse guarding the inner ward. The castle was held by Lord Grey, Lord Marcher of Dyffryn Clwyd, whose claim to fame was his acquiring, by devious means, the Dee estates of Owain Glyndwr. During Glyndwr's uprising, Ruthin Castle and town became a prime target. The castle was not captured, but the town was burned. Two years later, Glyndwr's forces defeated an English army at Vyrnwy and Lord Grey was imprisoned at Dolbadarn Castle. He was eventually released after a ransom had been paid.

Ruthin Castle played a prominent role in the English Civil War. After holding out during an earlier attack, it was besieged again in 1646 and finally surrendered to Major-General Mytton's Parliamentarian forces. The castle was destroyed and made uninhabitable after the war.

SKENFIRTH CASTLE, MONMOUTHSHIRE

This was one of the three castles built by the Normans to defend the borderland of Gwent. The castle was originally a motte and bailey built in the early twelfth century. However, a round keep surrounded by a four-sided curtain wall with five fortified towers was built in the early thirteenth century.

SWANSEA CASTLE, GLAMORGAN

This castle was built during the Normans' push across South Wales in 1099. A Norman knight, Henry Beaumont, captured the Gower and established a castle on the site. The original castle was no more than a wooden fortress and some stone structures. In the fourteenth century, Henry Gower, the Bishop of St David, built a substantial fortified manor house on part of the site. This structure consisted of several buildings, including a small round tower and a larger, four-sided tower. The original stronghold was often attacked by the Welsh. The bishop's fortified enclave was badly damaged in an attack by Owain Glyndwr in the fifteenth century.

TENBY CASTLE, PEMBROKESHIRE

This castle is located on cliff top on a small headland near the town with high cliffs on three sides. When the Normans invaded Wales, it was already the site of a small stronghold; they captured it at the beginning of the twelfth century. Because of the castle's position, the walls are very low, except on the landward side, where the gatehouse is located. The castle's strength lies in its D-shaped barbican with a small keep in the middle. The sturdy masonry walls and towers of the town's defences also protected it. The defences were continually upgraded and strengthened in 1457, and again in 1588 with the five-arched gates – a landmark in the town.

Like most other castles in Wales, the town and castle supported the Royalist cause during the English Civil War. It was twice bombarded by Parliamentarian warships and eventually surrendered in 1644. The town supported the Royalists again in 1648 but was defeated by Cromwell's forces, which left the castle walls in ruins.

TOMEN CASTLE, DOLWYDDELAN, GWYNEDD

This Welsh castle was built on a rocky site some five miles south-west of Betws y Coed. The rectangular tower dates back to the twelfth century.

TRETOWER CASTLE, BRECONSHIRE

This castle is situated a mile and a half from the town of Crickhowell. The original stronghold, built in around 1106, consisted of only a motte covered in stone facing. The castle was captured by the Welsh in 1233, and was recaptured soon afterwards. To improve its defence, a bailey was added with a stone wall and three towers, two of which formed the gate. A tall tower, or keep, was built in the middle of the motte. Over the next number of years, it withstood several attacks by Welsh forces. The castle passed into the possession of Sir Roger Vaughan, who

24. Tretower Castle. (*C. Thomas*)

in the fourteenth century built a fortified manor house to increase the castle's residential potential.

USK CASTLE, MONMOUTHSHIRE

This castle, dating from the twelfth century, is located in the town of Usk. It was built on an earlier Roman fortification by the de Clare family in the late twelfth century. The stronghold was captured by the Welsh in 1233, and again in 1265. Between 1212 and 1219, the castle was strengthened with an outer ward and a strong gatehouse. The D-shaped north-east tower and chapel were added in 1260. Further domestic buildings were built in the outer ward in the fifteenth century. According to the Welsh chronicles, Owain Glyndwr's forces captured the castle in 1403–04.

During the Civil War the castle were in the hands of the Royalist, but was subsequently captured and eventually destroyed by the Parliamentarians.

WELSHPOOL CASTLE, MONTGOMERYSHIRE

This was a simple motte-and-bailey castle, built mostly of timber, with a wooden tower built in the twelfth century. In 1196, it was captured by Norman forces, who mined beneath its foundations. However, the Welsh recaptured it soon afterwards. When the fortified manor of Powys Castle was established, the Welshpool site was abandoned.

WISTON CASTLE, PEMBROKESHIRE

Also known as Castell Gwis, Wiston Castle is situated some four miles outside Haverfordwest. It was built in the early twelfth century by Flemish settlers and consisted of a low motte and bailey with a polygonal shell wall on the motte. It was captured by the Welsh in 1147 and again in 1193, but was recaptured by the English in 1195. Its final battle was in 1220, when the castle was captured by Llywelyn the Great during his campaign in South Wales. For a brief period during the English Civil War, Royalists used the site as an outpost.

5

THE NEXT PHASE
IN DEFENCE

With the introduction of gunpowder into Europe from China in the middle of the thirteenth century, the art of warfare changed for good. It marked the beginning of a rethink in defence, especially in constructing fortifications.

The first cannon appeared on the continent at the beginning of the fourteenth century. It was not, perhaps, a reliable or safe implement, but it did propel a stone ball further than any slings or catapult in use.

The first cannons introduced in Britain were manufactured in Europe, but it was not long before wealthy individuals were manufacturing them locally, for use in defending castles. A certain rivalry emerged between aristocratic families, and therefore cannon designs and calibre got larger and more powerful. Private firms arose, manufacturing artillery pieces as well as gunpowder. It was not until the eighteenth century that the manufacturing of gunpowder and cannons was taken over by the state.

During the wars of the fifteenth century, it soon became apparent that a simple cannon ball could cause considerable damage to castle walls. Several castles in Wales were regarded as impregnable, capable of withstanding any siege or attack. However, during the English Civil War, this notion was put to the test when the Parliamentarians began using large siege guns.

Defence designers realised that all future fortifications had to be constructed much lower, with no high towers or buildings. The walls had to be either stone- or brick-built, backed by impact-absorbing earthen banks and keeping the wide, deep moats and ditches associated with the castles of old. These new structures came to be known as forts or blockhouses.

Some castles and fortifications in Wales were eventually adapted to take cannons and other hand-held guns. Arrow slits in towers were widened and the battlements were also modified to accommodate a cannon on a trolley. A good example, with dual arrow slits and gun ports, is Raglan Castle, the last of the old design built in the country. It was during the reign of Henry VIII that several castles were strengthened.

A great number of artillery fortifications were built around Britain, and these became known as 'Henry's Great Castles'. His plan involved constructing a chain of forts, blockhouses and gun batteries around the coast to protect ports and harbours. Several coastal areas that were potential landing beaches and inlets for the enemy were also earmarked for this defence. In his early years, Henry had travelled widely in Europe. He had seen different methods of defence and had studied warfare. He adapted much of what he saw into his programme for the defence of the realm.

These fortifications were the first serious defence development in Wales since Edward I's castle-building programme of the thirteenth century. The towers were reduced in height, with corner platforms surrounding the tower and protected by a stone wall and earthen bank. Most of the towers were round, but the walls were constructed on an angle to deflect a cannon shot.

The majority of Henry's great castles were built around the Humber and Thames estuaries, the south coast and Cornwall – the parts of the country facing continental Europe. The second stage of construction concentrated on harbours and ports. The scheme was extended to include gun emplacements and fortifications to protect entrances to inlets and estuaries The two best examples of Henry's construction programme in Wales are the two blockhouses built in 1530 at Dale and Angle to protect the entrance to Milford Haven.

The coastal artillery battery emplacement consisted of a low stone wall and base for ten cannons situated on a clifftop overlooking the entrance to the harbour. Usually there were three buildings, two for accommodation and one as a magazine. Local militia usually manned these gun emplacements.

In the period between the Tudor dynasty and the English Civil War, there was very little development in fortifications, but larger, heavier, higher-calibre cannons were introduced to the country from Europe. By the time of the war, the castles of Edward I were found to be inadequate against modern weapons. The forts of Henry VIII fared much better. Although several castles held out for weeks and months against an attack, it was only the lack of food and water that made them give up.

Most of the new fortifications built during the English Civil War were classed as temporary, and consisted of raised mounds surrounded by deep ditches, with gun emplacements for four cannons at each corner. A low wall built of reeds or stone strengthened with timber provided protection. Wooden huts were situated inside the raised embankment for accommodation and magazines. Few examples were built in Wales, an exception being in 1643, when two fortified army camps were built close to the town of Milford Haven. The New Model Army became invincible; the castles of Wales crumbled, one by one.

6

The English Civil War

This part of the nation's history is perhaps the saddest of all. Although it is known as the English Civil War, it involved everyone in Ireland, Scotland and Wales.

During the English Civil War, the battles between Parliamentarian and Royalist forces involved mostly long sieges and constant bombardment of castles, walled towns and other fortified positions.

In Wales, both sides used the medieval castles extensively. Around thirty were involved in one way or another, some changing hands regularly. Others were involved in long sieges. Some castles were in ruins, with several of the buildings roofless, but their walls and gatehouses were still intact and were often used. Castles that had been left to ruin because of the owner's financial problems were soon repaired and became bases for the Royalist cause. Several castles were modified to include cannons on the battlements and in the towers; some had an earthen embankment built to deter an attack. Arrow slits in the bastions of Raglan, Carew and Manorbier castles were enlarged for the use of muskets and hand-held cannons.

Since the early seventeenth century, the nation had relied solely on a system of county and town militias. It had been the duty of every lord of the manor or wealthy individual to raise a local contingent to fight for the realm or defend the towns or castles. Over the years, especially in times of peace, the system was in turmoil as many landowners regarded spending money on soldiering in peacetime was a waste of resources. It was only a small number of wealthy individuals that kept standing armies, and, even then, it was only a few hundred soldiers. In 1642, the King gave instruction to the nobility in Wales to raise an infantry regiment to protect the royal cause. The King paid the cost of the new army with coinage melted down from the gentry's silverware. As the King had lost control of the Royal Mint in London, he established new mints throughout the country. The one located at Aberystwyth covered most of Wales.

There are only a few examples of major military construction in Wales. At Milford Haven in 1643 a Royalist engineer, Richard Steele, constructed a fortified army camp and artillery positions east of the town, with a clear view of the inlet. A similar encampment called Pill Fort was built to the west to protect the entrance. Both encampments were built of wood, with earthen embankments. Another was near Caerphilly Castle, where a substantial earthen embankment was built to house artillery units.

During the English Civil War, Wales predominately supported the Royalist cause. Only Pembroke Castle remained a Parliamentary stronghold throughout most of the conflict.

Although the castles of Wales were designed for a different era, they were still formidable fortifications against most artillery of the time. A frontal attack was very foolish, as the Parliamentarians found to their cost on a number of occasions. However, more subtle methods were found – Powis Castle, for example, was captured by the Parliamentarians after a raid by during the night in October 1644. In 1645, Chirk Castle was captured after the bribing of the sentries.

In 1644 and 1649, trenches and gun positions were built around Raglan and Montgomery castles to isolate them during a siege. Another method used was the placing of mines (barrels of gunpowder) underneath walls and towers, such as at Monmouth and Ruthin. Another, more dangerous, approach was to fix a petard (a small hand-held explosive) on a gate. This method was used during the night assault to gain entrance to Powis Castle. The most commonly used method of attack was an intense bombardment by various artillery pieces, followed by a frontal attack. This method was used to capture Chepstow Castle in 1645 and again, after it changed hands, in 1648. Many fell after a long and arduous siege with a great loss of life. The most difficult castle to capture was Harlech, which took nearly nine months. Its defenders had made sure they had ample supplies of food and water, as well as powder and ammunition. Harlech, being situated in a prominent position, was very difficult to approach. But prolonged bombardment had very little effect on some castles – Pembroke Castle and its town was constantly bombarded with very little effect.

Parliamentary forces only made modest advances in Wales at the beginning of the English Civil War. It was not until the capture of Montgomery Castle in September 1644 that the gates to the country seemed to have been opened. This important castle was located on a hilltop and was a gateway to the upper River Severn and, eventually, Mid-Wales. The castle owner, Lord Herbert of Chirbury, had declared himself neutral in the war, and initially refused to surrender, but eventually, after the gate had been blown down, he gave up. The castle was occupied by 500 Parliamentary troops.

The Royalists, determined to recapture the castle, arrived with nearly 4,000 men and a number of siege guns. Another 3,000 Parliamentarians were sent to relieve the castle garrison. Within sight of the castle walls, a fierce battle took place. The King's army was routed.

For a brief moment in 1644, most of South Wales' castles were in Royalist hands, but they were soon retaken by the Parliamentary forces. Castles in Pembrokeshire fell one by one, almost effortlessly. Only Laugharne, over the border in Carmarthenshire, held out, but it eventually fell after a week-long siege. The Parliamentary forces had shipped heavy artillery from London via the port of Milford Haven. Initially the bombardment was unsuccessful, as the artillery had been located too far from the castle and most of the cannon balls fell short. Eventually, the town's outer defences were captured and Parliamentary forces were able to move their artillery closer, causing considerable damage to the castle's outer bailey and walls. The threat to mine the walls prompted the Royalist garrison to surrender.

The Royalist cause in Wales was on the verge of disappearing in 1645–46, prompting the King to visit the region in July–August 1645. He stayed at Raglan Castle, which was the only Royalist stronghold left in that area.

In North Wales, all of Edward's castles were in Royalist hands, but they soon fell to the might and discipline of the Parliamentary forces. In October, Denbigh

25. During the English Civil War, several castles were modified for muskets. Note the gun-loops above the arrow-loops of the fourteenth century.

26. Pembroke Castle was a Parliamentarian stronghold during the English Civil War.

Castle surrendered after heavy bombardment directed at the Goblin Tower. The Parliamentary forces followed the coast to Conwy, which turned out to be a more difficult proposition because of its location. The garrison eventually surrendered after a siege lasting three months. Caernarfon Castle was recaptured after a brief siege. Harlech Castle was next on the list of Royalist strongholds to be captured. It surrendered in March 1647, signalling the end of the English Civil War in Wales.

The Second English Civil War of 1648–49 was an opportunity for the Welsh gentry to air their discontentment with Parliamentarian rule in South Wales. A rebellion took place and the castles and other fortifications were in the middle of another conflict. Many castles and towns still supported the Royalists, an example being Pembroke Castle, which surrendered after a seven-week siege. The Welsh Royalists were finally defeated at the Battle of St Fagans in May 1648. The final Royalist castle was at Chepstow; its fall brought an end to this futile war.

After the war, Parliament declared that all castles that took part in the war, especially on the Royalist side, were to be destroyed. Initially, gunpowder was

27. Raglan Castle was never restored after damage sustained during the English Civil War.

used, for example at Aberystwyth, completely destroying the structure. However, this method proved rather expensive, as it required a considerable amount of gunpowder, which the nation did not possess. Other methods, such as lighting fires under the foundation of the walls and turrets, were used. Eventually, it was decided to make the castles uninhabitable by removing all wooden features, including the floors.

Even the Restoration in 1660 did not end the decommissioning of the castles, as lead and timber were valuable commodities. Wood was stripped from the castles at Beaumaris, Conwy and Denbigh in North Wales. As the result, these majestic structures became homes for wild animals, cattle and sheep, and for the countless homeless families that wandered the country.

The English Civil War instigated rapid development in military tactics, especially a more mobile form of warfare utilising cavalry and towed artillery. Mobile 24-pounder siege guns, which could demolish the stone walls of a castle, were introduced. Only the addition of 15 feet of earth against the wall was sufficient to absorb an iron shot. Cannons of the period had an effective range of about a mile and a half. Therefore outer defences had to be built further out, and were usually armed with 5-pounder guns. Heavier cannons required firm stone ground or a specially built wooden platform.

28. Harlech was the last castle in Wales to surrender to Parliamentarian forces.

The days of the medieval castles as fortifications had come to an end, but many remain standing today as a symbol of a long-gone era. Most town and city walls have been demolished; the stone was used for building new homes and other buildings.

7

EIGHTEENTH-CENTURY FORTIFICATIONS

During the period of unrest between the English Civil War and the Jacobite Risings, there was hardly any development of fortifications in Wales. Most castles and fortified positions there were either demolished or made uninhabitable. In England and Scotland, priority was given to repairing the existing fortifications and constructing new ones.

The next phase of coastal defence in Wales occurred in the eighteenth century, when France was considered the country's main threat.

With Britain siding with the Protestant cause in Europe, repercussions were inevitable. With the accession of William of Orange to the English throne, Britain became allied to the Dutch cause against France, resulting in two long wars, the war of the Grand Alliance (1689–97) and the War of the Spanish Succession (1701–14). It was in 1740, during the War of the Austrian Succession (1740–48), that the French attempted an invasion of Britain, which was foiled by a severe storm in the English Channel.

The Royal Navy and other shipping had always used the sheltered waters of Milford Haven. In 1748, years before the French invasion at Fishguard, plans to build a gun fort to protect Paterchurch (Pembroke Dock) and the inner inlet were put forward. Work on Pater Fort – as it was known – began in 1750. It is located on the north-western corner of the dockyard, near Carr Jetty. The fort was constructed of timber and limestone, complete with sturdy barracks for its defenders. By 1759, the threat of invasion during the Seven Years' War (1756–63) had passed; further construction was suspended. Throughout the various conflicts, one of France's main aims was to invade the British Isles.

During the American War of Independence (1775–83) the French sided with the colonists, not because they particularly supported the cause, but it was an opportunity to 'have go' at Britain.

The French assisted the colonists in various ways during their land campaign, and on the high seas. In 1778, the American adventurer John Paul Jones attacked and destroyed a shore battery at Whitehaven in Cumbria with French assistance. This incident and the continuous invasion threat caused alarms in Britain, especially in the English Channel regions. Other areas, especially on the Welsh coast, were classed as vulnerable to enemy attack from the sea.

The defences built in the Tudor period around Milford Haven and the Severn Estuary had been neglected. Stone walls and buildings were crumbling away. These areas, with their naval and mercantile ports, dockyards, sheltered anchorages and various harbours, were of great importance to the British.

Since it did not lie on the English Channel, the Welsh coastline was considered a safe area for shipping. Therefore, all rebuilding of coastal defences was concentrated in the Channel area and East Anglia, areas facing the Continent.

The French Revolutionary Wars began in 1792; they were the beginning of more or less twenty years of conflict between Britain and France. The threat of an invasion was constant, so the Government ordered immediate work on constructing new fortifications. In 1796, Spain, an ally of France, declared war on Britain, which added to the concern of the nation. The first attempted invasion was mounted by the Spaniards at Bantry Bay in Ireland, followed by a second attempt in 1798. Both were unsuccessful.

In 1797, a small French force under the command of an Irish-American, Colonel William Tate, left Brest for England, flying a Russian flag. The invasion force consisted of 600 regular troops and 800 convicts released from French prisons to fight for France, as well as nearly a hundred émigrés captured at Quiberon, in Canada. The original plan was to land near Bristol, with instructions to burn the town and cause mayhem in the surrounding area. Due to poor navigation and bad weather, the plan was a failure from the start. An alternative plan to land troops in the Cardigan Bay area and march through Wales to Chester and Liverpool, gathering disillusioned Welshmen, was considered.

As the four ships – *La Resistance*, *La Constance*, *La Vengeance* and the *Vautor* – neared British waters, they flew a British flag to confuse local defences. The four French ships anchored off Carreg Wastad Point with the intention of landing at Fishguard, but after having been fired on by the coastal battery they decided that the town was too heavily defended. Only one blank shot was fired, as the garrison did not have any cannonballs and the powder was too damp to be used. Colonel Tate ordered his men to land at Carreg Wastad, a few miles away. Seventeen boatloads of troops and supplies were landed on the shore. After spending hours scaling a high cliff and rocky shoreline with forty-seven barrels of gunpowder and twelve boxes of grenades, the men eventually established a base camp. After pillaging some local farms and acquiring local brew, several of the invading French got drunk and were captured by the local people, led by heroine Jemima Nicholas. The Pembroke Fencibles and the

Cardiganshire Militia led by Lord Cawdor rounded up the rest of the invasion force over the next few days. On 9 March, Royal Navy ships HMS *St Fiorenzo* and HMS *Nymph* pursued the invasion fleet, encountering first *La Resistance*, which had been crippled by the bad weather in the Irish Sea. *La Constance* was also encountered and, after a brief skirmish, both French ships surrendered. *La Resistance* was re-fitted and renamed HMS *Fisgard*, while *La Constance* was renamed HMS *Constance*. This was the last attempted invasion of Britain.

The whole story is told in the Fishguard Tapestry, which was made by local people to commemorate the 200th anniversary of the invasion. It is on display in the town hall.

Invasion was possible, even with coastal fortification, as so much of the coast in the United Kingdom was unprotected and desolate.

With the opening of the Royal Dockyard at Pembroke Dock in 1815, there was an urgent case for defence of Milford Haven. The Admiralty used two-thirds of the area occupied by the Pater Battery for the dockyard, so a new fortified battery was needed. Only some work was done at Pater Fort in 1830 and the fort was only partially garrisoned a year later. The fort was rebuilt in 1840–42 to provide protection for the dockyard. The battery consisted of twenty-three guns and was only finally dismantled in 1903.

During the Napoleonic Wars there were threats of invasion, which prompted the Government to hold an urgent review of coastal defences, especially on the south and east coasts of Britain. The failed invasion at Fishguard in 1797 prompted the authorities to include West Wales in their review. In 1803, a scheme was put in action to build a chain of military supporting towers mounting cannons, accommodation for troops, and an armoury. These towers came to be known as Martello Towers and were built between 1803 and 1860. The design originated during the French Revolutionary War in Corsica in 1794, when a sixteenth-century stone tower held by the French at Martello Point held out against an overwhelming British force for two days. Constant bombardment from ships and shore batteries had little effect on the structure, as cannon balls tended to ricochet off the round towers.

No Martello Towers were built in Wales, although several medieval towers were modified to house their artillery pieces on their roofs or accommodate a small garrison, mostly for look-out purposes. The two gun towers built at Pembroke Dock in 1849 were very similar to the Martello Towers.

8

PALMERSTON'S FOLLIES

The next interesting phase in the development of fortifications in Wales was when the Duke of Wellington (then the Prime Minister) pushed a more effective coastal defence proposal through Parliament in order to reduce the burden on the army and navy. He understood the pressure on the two services to fight wars on the Continent and elsewhere without having to provide a home defence. Yet he was adamant that the army would be used to protect ports and estuaries as well as the capital city. Other areas and coastlines would be protected by a series of new fortifications manned by local yeomanry overseen by experienced officers.

Lord Palmerston had often expressed in Parliament that France might still attempt an invasion across the Channel with the fast steamships that were being introduced into its navy. But even with constant scaremongering from a number of individuals, only modest changes were made to coastal defence, and that was mostly in Southern England.

France was always considered the main enemy of Britain, influencing other nations on the Continent and beyond. There was a real fear of an invasion in 1851–52, when the French seemed to be massing troops and ships in the Channel ports and estuaries. The surprise invasion at Fishguard in 1797 was always in politicians' minds, and coastal fortifications once again became an important agenda. The Government reacted by finding more money to update fortification designs and soon began building new forts. Three areas were considered for new fortifications – the approaches to Portsmouth, the island of Alderney, and Milford Haven in Pembrokeshire.

At Milford Haven in 1841, a defensible, bastioned barrack was built as part of the landward defence of the dockyard at Pembroke Dock. An army garrison manned this barrack.

Other new fortifications were also rushed through at great speed. Two new forts were built on a small island and rocks in the Haven – Stack Rock, which became operational in 1851, and the larger Thorn Island, established in 1852 at the height of the invasion threat.

The Government placed great importance in Milford Haven. Four years later, a fort was built at Dale and the West Blockhouse was eventually completed. There were two reasons for the development of the defences at Milford Haven – firstly to defend the docks and the naval shipyard, and secondly to deny the enemy use of the sheltered estuary for anchorage or for mounting an invasion.

Two lines of defence were built behind the three forts, West Blockhouse, Dale and Thorn Island. The first was the build-up of defences at Stack Rock fort, supplemented by the shore batteries at Chapel Bay and South Hook Point. The second line of defence involved the forts at Hubberston and Popton and the defensible barracks at Pembroke Dock. The two gun towers protecting the naval shipyard were re-gunned. It seems that Pembroke Castle was considered as in the line of defence at one time, but it was dropped as it required considerable development. The forts never fired a gun in anger and many regarded them as an expensive venture. Several thousand troops – regular and yeomanry – manned the forts and gun emplacements. However, they were a deterrent and the population felt protected.

In June 1859, Lord Palmerston became Prime Minister. He had for a number of years questioned Britain's defences, and he had always been suspicious of French intentions. As Prime Minister he had more of an opportunity to declare his concern for the nation's coastal defences, as they had not been kept up to date with the development of foreign naval ships and gunnery. In August 1859, he appointed a Royal Commission to look into coastal defences around most of the sensitive areas of the British Isles.

A year later, the Royal Commission on the Defence of the United Kingdom was published and two of the areas highlighted were Milford Haven and the Bristol Channel.

THE BRISTOL CHANNEL

The sole purpose of the Bristol Channel defences was to protect the western ports of Bristol in the West Country, Barry, Cardiff and Newport in South Wales. The Severn Estuary was regarded as an important seaway into the heartland of Britain. Like Milford Haven, the area faced away from Continental Europe and had been regarded as safe, but it became apparent that a determined enemy would try to land a force or attack these valuable areas. This was proven in 1797, when the French landed at Fishguard.

For protection, gun batteries were built at Avonmouth and Portishead to defend the river mouth. The 1860 Royal Commission proposed a series of new

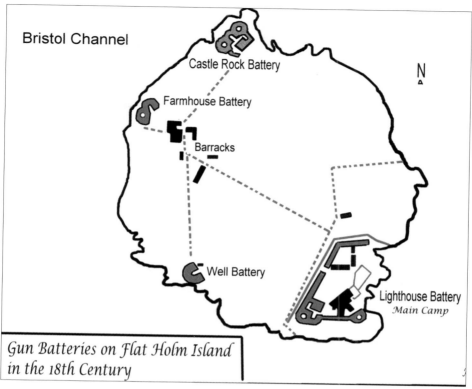

Bristol Channel

Castle Rock Battery

Farmhouse Battery

Barracks

N

Well Battery

Lighthouse Battery
Main Camp

Gun Batteries on Flat Holm Island in the 18th Century

29. Layout plan of gun emplacements on Flat Holm.

batteries on the islands of Steep Holm and Flat Holm in the middle of the Bristol Channel. These were supplemented by the batteries at Brean Down Fort on the English side, and Lavernock Point and Penarth Head on the Welsh side. A small fort was built near the lighthouse on a rocky islet at Mumbles in 1860 before the recommendation of the Royal Commission report was published. The fort was armed with five 80-pounder smoothbore guns manned by a small company of men.

The batteries covered all entrances in and out of the Bristol Channel and the Severn Estuary. Most of the batteries were issued with the new 7-inch rifled muzzle-loading (RML) guns on Moncrieff carriages. Work on fortifying Steep Holm began in 1866. Initially the base housed four batteries of 7-inch RML guns, but they were replaced by the newer and more effective Armstrong 6-inch RML guns, which had been specially designed for coastal defence. A stone barrack block was constructed to accommodate over fifty men, together with an underground tank providing drinking water for the soldiers. An earth-covered magazine was also part of the construction.

30. A typical gun casement common to forts and gun emplacements.

Defences on Flat Holm were built in conjunction with Steep Holm, with builders moving between the two islands. Here four batteries of nine 7-inch guns on Moncrieff carriages were built, together with a barrack for around fifty soldiers and the usual earth-covered ammunition store. The camp layout on both islands was nearly identical. The Flat Holm batteries were upgraded to house the 6-inch Armstrong guns in 1903, and remained operational during the First World War. The inventor Marconi used the facility at Flat Holm in May 1897 when he sent a message by wireless telegraphy between the island and Lavernock Point on the Welsh mainland.

MILFORD HAVEN

The other area in Wales that caused great concern to the Government was Milford Haven, with its port, naval shipyard and sheltered anchorage for shipping. Due to continuous unrest on the Continent, especially in France, the possibility of yet another war and the threat of invasion was inevitable. The Government realised that most of the nation's Royal Dockyards were vulnerable to attack from the sea. There had not been any improvements or new fort construction at Milford Haven since the construction of two blockhouses at the entrance of the inlet during the reign of Henry VIII in 1580.

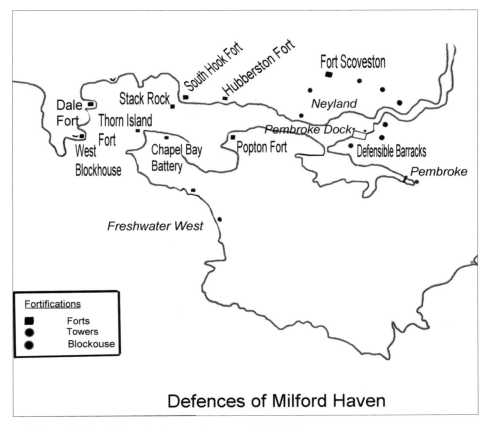

31. Map of Milford Haven's nineteenth-century fortifications.

The Admiralty was constantly looking for locations to establish a naval shipyard, preferably away from the prying eyes of the French. In 1813, the town of Paterchurch, which later became known as Pembroke Dock, was chosen. It is located on the inlet known as Milford Haven. Wales' only Royal Dockyard was opened in 1815, with the first warship being launched on 10 February 1816. Even a naval study a year later pointed out that protection of the dockyard was very weak and recommended building at least three gun towers and a series of artillery batteries on either side of Milford Haven. However, Napoleon had been beaten two years earlier at Waterloo, and the French would not be able to mount any sort of an attack for years to come. All plans for fortifying the area were abandoned.

The next plan for fortification came about as the result of a concern about a landward attack, as a determined enemy could land anywhere on the Pembrokeshire coast and march across the county. In 1841, fortified defensible barracks were built to house a detachment of Royal Marines, whose task was to

32. A 9-inch rifled muzzle-loaded gun emplacement.

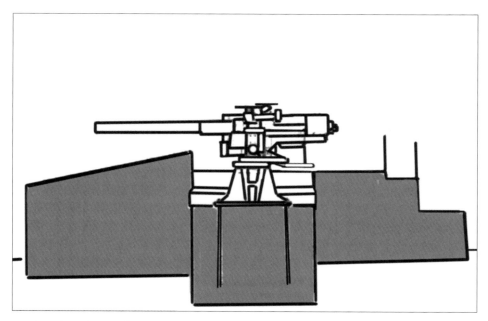

33. Drawing of a 6-inch BL MK VIII gun on a CPIvI Mounting emplacement.

protect the dockyard. There was considerable unrest in Europe in 1848, which became known as the Year of the Revolution. The Palmerston government watched the events unfolding on the Continent, especially in France, with great interest. Once again there was concern about the defence of key areas.

Two gun towers were built between 1848 and 1850 on either side of the shipyard – North East Gun Tower and South West Gun Tower. Another tower capable of housing three 12-pounder artillery pieces was built on Stack Rock, near the entrance of Milford Haven.

Fortification continued between 1850 and 1857 with the building of forts on Thorn Island, at Dale, and on the site of Henry VIII's West Blockhouse. A committee was appointed by the Government to assess the defensive structures at Milford Haven and Pembroke Dock. It recommended two lines of fortifications, as mentioned earlier in the chapter. All the recommendations were carried out.

In 1859, work began on the forts at South Hook and Popton. The fort at Stack Rock was strengthened with an enclosed, curved casement battery. As soon as one fortification was completed, another began. In 1861, work began on Fort Scoveston, slightly inland in an elevated position, but with a clear view of Milford Haven and Pembroke Dock. Chapel Bay battery was another fortification built as the result of Royal Commission. At the end of the fortification programme there were seven forts, one battery emplacement, two gun towers and a defensible barrack, which was a fort in its own right. All the defences were able to crossfire with each other, and therefore they covered every inch of waterway. Most of the work was completed by the middle of 1870, but with the introduction of the rifled cannons all artillery pieces were declared obsolete. This development meant that design of these fortifications was rendered obsolete as well, which led to the remodelling of parts of the forts and the gun batteries.

Additional forts were proposed to protect the landward approach to Milford Haven and the Royal Dockyard. They were to be located at Pennar Farm, Bush Corner, Ferry Hill, Waterston, Honeyborough, Barnlake, Scoveston, Newton and Burton. The total cost of the forts was huge, and it was money the Treasury was not prepared to give. Therefore, only a fort at Scoveston was completed. It was not armed. Milford Haven is very unique as its defences were built in one period only; even then, the designs of the fortifications varied.

OTHER AREAS IN WALES

Another area of concern was around Tenby, which was a potential landing place for an enemy force. The Royal Commission on the Defence of the United Kingdom recommended that six forts be built along the coast to defend potential landing places on Caldey Island, Lydstep, Freshwater East Freshwater West and Tenby. However, only one fort was constructed – on

St Catherine Island (Ynys Catrin), in the shadow of the twelfth-century Tenby Castle. The fort was design by Lieutenant-Colonel William Jervois, Deputy Director of Fortifications. Work began in 1867.

There is only one example of such forts in North Wales – Fort Belan on the Dinlle Peninsula, overlooking the southern entrance to the Menai Straits. During the American War of Independence, American ships – with the help of the French – were harassing British ships around the British Isles. American privateers preyed on shipping sailing the North Wales coast to Liverpool, as well as the Holyhead–Dublin ferries. Thomas Wynn, then the local Member of Parliament and the Constable of Caernarfon, was concerned that the Menai Straits would be attacked or invaded. With his own money, he built a fort on the tip of the peninsula and manned it with his own men. For his patronage and efforts, he was awarded a peerage. During the Napoleonic Wars, the fortress became one of a chain of forts in the country. It was later included in Palmerston's Royal Commission plans for defence of the coastline.

34. Aerial photograph of Tenby with its castle and fort.

GLOSSARY

bailey: a defended courtyard contained by the outer wall of a castle

barbican: the strong defensive tower of a castle or a walled town

bastion: a projecting part of a wall, rampart or fortification

boom defence: a chain or cable barrier stretched across a waterway

calibre: the diameter of the bore of a gun

caponier: a small, single- or double-storey structure providing embraces for cannons and muskets

casements: chambers in a structure containing gun positions

constable: a title for the governor, warden or captain of a castle

curtain: a wall that encloses a bailey or a ward

donjon: a large tower or keep; a fortified central tower

keep: a stronghold or the innermost fortified part of a castle

magazine: a fortified room or building in a fort or battery for storing gunpowder and ammunition

motte: the mound on which a castle is built

murder holes: openings in the roof and side walls of an enclosed passageway where attackers could be ambushed

petard: a large charge of explosive for attaching to gates during sieges

portcullis: a heavy iron gate that slides vertically

postern: a small door or gate set a distance from the main entrance; often obscured and hidden

pounder: cannons were referred to according to the weight of the projectile it could fire

rampart: a high bank

turret towers: small half-towers on outer castle walls and town walls

ward: an open area within the castle walls

Acknowledgements

I would like to thank the following people and organisations for their assistance with the writing of this book: Anglesey Maritime Museum; Cadw; Lyn Carter; Nick Catford; Coflein; Conwy County Borough Council Archives; Dale Fort Field Centre; Dyfed Archaeological Trust; Fort Belan, Gwyned; G. Evans; Guntower Museum, Pembroke Dock; Haverfordwest Museum; Imperial War Museum; Professor A. T. Jones; National Museum of Wales; Benjamin Owens; Palmerston Forts Society; Pembrokeshire County Council; Nerys Phillips; Sian Phillips; Tenby Museum; Jeffrey L. Thomas (author, Castles of Wales); various libraries throughout Wales; and the Welsh Assembly Government.

I would also like to thank the members of my family who have assisted me in taking photographs of the Welsh castles and fortifications. Various other organisations and historical groups have provided invaluable information.